Educate 1-to-1

Dominic Norrish
Mark Baker
Daniel Edwards
José Picardo
Adam Webster

CONTENTS

1 INTRODUCTION

Hello! Welcome. Please sit down, I have some bad news and I'm afraid you're not going to like it very much.

Most technological interventions in education fail. They fail through poor design, flawed implementation or, most commonly, unsuccessful attempts to change the way teachers do things. Statistically speaking, there's a high chance that your own bold project will founder on the rocky coast of Wireless Dismay or be dashed against the harsh cliffs of Educators' Indifference.

This is a shame as, for the most part, these interventions (and yours particularly, I'm sure) would improve learning and teaching if they stuck. It's also a shame as, for the most part, these causes of failure are foreseeable and can be overcome with access to good advice. Often all they are missing is a trusted lighthouse and an experienced pilot.

The approach of giving every child their own mobile, converged and highly functional computer - 1-to-1 in shorthand - promises more than any edtech innovation that has come before because it is predicated on the empowerment of the learner and the integration of technology into the process of learning, not as a thing in and of itself. According to BESA's 2013 report1, 57% of Primaries and 75% of Secondaries plan on implementing a one-device-per-child strategy in the next few years.

Yet many schools are still struggling to make it work, for the same reasons as ever, despite the cost, the potential and the risks that attend a failed project of this scale. For anyone with a passion for technology's ability to propel children towards success, this is unacceptable. 1-to-1 isn't interactive whiteboards or flipcams - it is actually something that can really change lives if done well. It shouldn't be allowed to fail.

This book is aimed at increasing your chances of successfully designing, implementing and sustaining a 1-to-1 programme in your school. It brings together the collective experience of five veteran 1-to-1 educators who have done the failing on your behalf. Sometimes repeatedly. It contains all those hard-won lessons but none of the pain of working out what doesn't work.

Adam, Daniel, José, Mark and I have written this book in order that our overlapping expertise and experience can help many other schools achieve the impact we've seen in our own institutions through the discerning application of 1-to-1.

Dominic

---

[1] http://www.besa.org.uk/sites/default/files/tab2013_0.pdf

2 VISIONING

Section 2.1 The importance of making the educational case

Possibly the most important (certainly the first) question to ask any school considering whether to implement a 1-to-1 strategy is 'why?'. There are many good reasons why such a strategy would be desirable for most schools, and we will be exploring them below, but there are also other arguments that are often put forward as a *justification* for 1-to-1 implementations that would be shallow, short-term and ultimately self-defeating motivations. There is, in fact, only one reason why any school should ever do this, and that's because it will help children to learn. This is the reason why it is absolutely vital that you start by working out where, if anywhere, 1-to-1 fits in your educational vision.

No school should embark on a project of this scale unless it is going to significantly help to achieve educational objectives. If your starting point is '1-to-1 is the answer, what's the question again?' you should probably rethink your priorities. Whilst the side benefits to marketing are very real, they cannot be the driving force behind your 1-to-1 project. You shouldn't do this because the school down the road is, you should do this because you've considered the educational benefits, weighed up the cost of change and have decided it's in the interests of the children in your care.

There's a reason why it's not a good idea to just plough ahead without making the educational case, and it's because without going through this important process, and being public about it, the school's teachers will quickly realise that the project is a gimmick. It'll be obvious to them because there will be no passion. The huge amount of time and political capital that's needed to make the change stick (the training, the piloting, the side-lining of other initiatives) won't be invested. Sooner or later they will see through the thin veneer of seriousness, and they'll treat it with the respect it deserves. In short, they won't waste their time or risk their students' futures with what they may perceive to be a vanity project.

Too often engagement and the 'wow factor' are relied upon as the principal reasons for adopting mobile devices. The thinking is that students find the use of mobile technology appealing and that this will result in wider engagement and greater achievement in learning. Whilst this may well be true in the short term, students quickly return to the original levels of engagement in the long term as the wow factor ebbs away, as anyone who has used mobile devices or Internet tools to support teaching and learning would attest. Engagement and wowing, therefore, ought not to be the principal reasons to propound a 1-to-1 implementation. So, if appealing to students' preferences alone is not a good enough reason, what is?

The simple answer has to be to support, facilitate and enhance the processes involved in teaching and learning. When articulating a 1-to-1 vision to teachers, students, parents and the wider school community, it is absolutely essential to focus on this. The success of any strategy will be judged ultimately on whether the 1-to-1 implementation had a positive impact on the educational outcomes for students. Should we ignore student engagement? No, engagement and motivation should certainly be taken into account, but as part of a wider strategy in which supporting teaching and learning is prioritised, whilst always remembering that what students find engaging can but does not always result in better teaching or learning.

When focusing on how mobile technology would impact teaching and learning, a good place to start would be the classroom. Research shows that lessons are most effective when they are structured thus:

- An initial review of prior knowledge
- A formal presentation
- Guided practice
- Initial feedback
- Independent practice
- A follow-up review

(Hattie and Yates 2014)[2]

It could be easily argued that all of these aspects of a lesson can be supported and, in some instances, improved by the application of technology. From this perspective, a 1-to-1 vision ought to take into account how lessons are most effective and put in place the means and support to enable teachers to use technology in such a way that the quality of teaching and learning in their lessons is enhanced by its use, when it is possible and appropriate. And it may not always be so!

Section 2.2 Mapping mobile learning affordances to known success strategies

A really good approach to working out how 1-to-1 is going to have educational impact is to start with what we know and spread technology on top of that, as an accelerant. For example, Hattie's research has demonstrated that one of the most useful things a teacher can do to support learning is to provide high-quality, timely and on-going feedback to students. So, knowing this, could we ask the question of how technology could deepen, speed up and generally make this process stick better?

According Gareth Mills, Head of Learning and Innovation at Futurelab, "by creating a matrix with 'effective pedagogy' (across the top) and 'uses of technology' (down the side) it is possible to consider how we might think about the intersections as areas of activity most likely to yield positive results"[3]. By zooming in on the different learning affordances, rather than

---

[2] Hattie, J. and Yates, G. (2014) Visible learning and the science of how we learn. Oxon: Routledge

applying a wide lens that tends to view technology as a separate entity and not an intrinsic aspect of teaching and learning today, we can begin to identify proven strategies that help us draw a route map for the integration of mobile technology into the daily business of teaching and learning, thus maximising its potential in education. Keri Facer, Professor of Educational & Social Futures at the University of Bristol, agrees on the need to "move away from the dominant view of mobile learning as an isolated activity to explore mobile learning as a rich, collaborative and conversational experience, whether in classrooms, homes or the streets of a city."[4]

This philosophy is beginning to be applied in academic studies and research, such as that of the University of Hull[5], which took a more inclusive approach and looked at how tablets were being used in eight schools and six local authorities across Scotland. The study looked specifically into: how tablet devices impact on teaching and learning; the leadership and management issues associated with the deployment of mobile devices in schools and local authorities; parental engagement with learning when students use mobile technologies as personal devices; and professional development and learning for teachers introducing personal mobile devices into the curriculum. Its key findings were:

1. Use of tablet devices such as the iPad was found to facilitate the achievement of many of the core elements required within the Curriculum for Excellence framework and could be further developed in order to achieve these aspirations.
2. The adoption of a personalised device such as an iPad significantly transforms access to and use of technology inside the classroom with many attendant benefits.
3. Personal 'ownership' of the device is seen as the single most important factor for successful use of this technology.

---

[3] Presentation given to United Learning Leadership Conference, Leeds, March 2014
[4] Naismith, L. et al. (2004) Literature review in mobile technologies and learning. Bristol: Futurelab
[5] Burden, K. et al. (2012) iPad Scotland Evaluation. Hull: University of Hull

4. The individual possession of and early familiarisation with the iPad by teachers was seen as being responsible for the significant 'buy in' and low level of resistance from teachers.

5. As a result of the pilot initiative schools are reconsidering their existing technology deployments with a view to more mobile provision.

6. The device is bringing about significant changes in the way teachers approach their professional role as educators and is changing the way they see themselves and their pedagogy.

7. Parents also appear to become more engaged with the school and their child's learning when the iPad travels home with the student.

8. Education departments and associated services within Local Authorities were perceived to have been helpful towards the iPad initiative and to have worked hard to support its use although corporate systems sometimes found this challenging.

9. Many teachers and students wish to have access to the iPad after the end of the trial and are convinced it has changed learning for the better.

Analysis of the evidence base and expert academic opinion allow us to surmise that mobile technologies can indeed have a potentially sizeable and positive effect on children's learning outcomes, especially when we look at how mobile technologies support the processes of, and provide affordances for, teaching and learning. Therefore, a much better case for adoption of mobile technologies can be made by viewing technology through this lens, rather than by looking at technology as a single measurable intervention, as is the case in most of the current research and evidence base.

Section 2.3 Finally, a panacea to every education ill, in one shiny box!

There is a great variety of digital tools that claim to support teaching and learning, some of which are more effective than others. Too often, teachers are presented with tools that portray a particular technology as a magic solution to all their problems. It is not. This *silver bullet* portrayal of technology has done much harm to teachers' perceptions and has created large pockets of vociferous cynicism, quite a lot of which is not sufficiently well-informed. Through a clear 1-to-1 vision, teachers need an informed voice that can guide them past this cynicism, as well as any unsubstantiated enthusiasm, towards technologies that can really make a positive impact to outcomes for their students.

When articulating your 1-to-1 vision to colleagues, including senior leadership, we would suggest it is essential to remain firmly grounded on what has been shown to work first, so that they can then more easily envision future potential of mobile technologies. Don't assume that because you can see A leading to B leading C, that everyone else will. Your colleagues will rightly be suspicious of unsubstantiated claims regarding the potential of technology, especially if all they hear is second-hand accounts of what the 1-to-1 vision entails. In order to avoid this, you might consider bringing on board a significant number of colleagues as early as possible, so that they can contribute to designing and fleshing out the vision and act as your ambassadors to the staff room. Bringing colleagues on board with a range of experience, encompassing both academic and pastoral responsibilities, can help translate this vision and ensure that their different perspectives ultimately contribute to develop that vision into a successful strategy.

With this 1-to-1 team in place, you can begin to explore jointly ways in which mobile devices can support classroom practice. Depending on the experience and disposition of your colleagues, you may need to plant a few seeds as to what best practice using mobile devices in the classroom looks like, but we would encourage you to allow your colleagues to experiment, learn from their own experiences and come up with their own ideas. This, of course, can only be achieved if your colleagues have access to mobile devices well before the students, so that they feel more confident in their use by the time the students begin to rock up to lessons carrying mobile technology in their school bags. We will explore suggested timings and stages of the 1-to-1 implementation later on in Sections 3.2 & 7.1

2.3.1 Carrying out a SWOT analysis with students

At the same time that you are doing this, you might also want to consider getting your students involved so that they understand that a 1-to-1 implementation remains deeply grounded in supporting the teaching and the learning that goes on in your school. This would also have the advantage of helping staff see why their pupils would value access to mobile learning.

There appears to exist a damaging misconception that students these days are *digital natives* and that this means that they will immediately understand how to use technology to further their academic achievement. In fact, most students will associate mobile technologies - tablets and mobile phones in particular - with gaming and other leisure and social activities and will not immediately see what benefits a 1-to-1 environment will bring to their education. Your students are simply not used to using digital technologies in the classroom environment and many will view technology more as a hindrance and a distraction than a helpful addition. Carrying out a SWOT analysis might be a way to quickly ascertain how students feel about mobile technology before any implementation is carried out. When one of the authors carried out a SWOT analysis with a representative sample of 23 students from year 6 to year 13, the verbatim results were as follows:

STRENGTHS	WEAKNESSES
•Helps you to research topics – internet •More organised filing system •Keeps you updated on news – personal message system? •Can link subjects •Quick and easy to check MIS messages and emails •Saving documents all into the same folders and easy to access at home •Only need iPad and don't need all the books which make bags really heavy •Don't have to get out laptops for research •Will motivate students more •It is easier to carry around, and you have it all the time •You would have your planner and calendar etc so it will be easier to use •You can take screenshots of your homework so you don't lose it •Saves paper •Easily access files from school at home •You can watch educational videos •Digital textbooks •Suits more ways of learning •Use in English lessons – possible to have books on tablets •Helps with homework management •Online planner •Things you can do on iPads but not on computers •Don't have to carry around books and loose sheets •You don't have to worry about losing sheets and homework	•Over-reliance on tablets – not using books, library, other resources •How will teachers mark the work? •Autocorrect and won't know about spelling •Makes things harder when doing a test because of switching between writing and typing •A disadvantage of mobile technology outside the classroom is that you may not have any WIFI •Running out of charge •iMessage and FaceTime •Can just slide it up and take pictures •Sometimes quicker to do something with pen and paper •May not be locked •Technology needs constant maintenance – updating and short life spans •Notes could get wiped •Technology can be temperamental •Whether they'd get their use •Technology needs constant updating •Will teachers use them? •People cheating on tests •Temptation and using them inappropriately •Some subjects lend themselves more naturally than others •May become a distraction during lesson and homework time
OPPORTUNITIES	THREATS
•Interactive learning •More organised – an online planner? •Dictionary •PowerPoints for classes •Online diagrams for sciences •The opportunities for teaching and learning across different subjects are that, for example, you do not know the meaning of "anti-social" and neither did your teacher; you could use your phone, iPad or tablet •Educational games •Listen to music •Links to School system •Some people work better on iPads as they are more used to them at home •You can access all your work anywhere •Timetable/homework diary •Homework •You can take it home •Textbooks on iPad •Independent learning and research •More creative ways to present ideas •Suits a wider variety of learning skills •You might save time •Checking emails and pupil messages •Sharing resources •Easy access to online materials	•Students could get distracted during lessons •Internet sites could be irrelevant •Classroom management •WIFI signal •When connected to the school WIFI, block Facebook, Twitter etc. But please don't do the educational filter on YouTube as you can literally watch no videos! •You can set up their FaceTime account and contact people •Battery life •Social media sites – though they can be be blocked •Get distracted during lessons •Can be broken or lost •Using iPads at break can be anti-social •If too used to typing –what will happen in exam? •If we're too dependent on technology what will happen in exams when we have no auto-correct? •English spellcheck/grammar •Camera used to take selfies •Cheating in Google Translate •Classroom management – increase in sanctions •Plagiarism: People cheating using website answers

Upon scrutiny of these responses two things become obvious. Firstly, any intrinsic motivation or desire to use technology is tempered by the students' own concerns and, secondly, these concerns actually mirror pretty closely those of the adults in their charge. We can quickly glean that students can be as conservative as adults, if not more, and that children do not necessarily know better when it comes to technology just because they have grown up surrounded by it.

In this particular case, the advantages, as perceived by the students, boil down to the access to and the creation of multimedia resources, whereas the perceived disadvantages mostly revolve around practical issues (such as charging, breakages or loss) and behaviour (such as disruption, plagiarism and distraction). Most interesting of all is how students tend to view the potential of the social Internet to turbo-charge communication as more of a threat than an opportunity. However, remember that this analysis reflects a single school's context and that your students may come to different, though still informative, conclusions.

Carrying out this this simple yet illuminating SWOT analysis allowed one of the authors' schools to take these views into account and put together a programme of lunchtime meetings and workshops in which colleagues and students took part and sought to address any concerns or fears - founded or unfounded. In these workshops students and teachers contributed to the creation of an Acceptable User Agreement (AUP) and suggested additions and alterations to our rewards and sanctions policy, thus helping us to mitigate potentially damaging ill-conceived attitudes and misconceptions from the outset.

Later on, as the 1-to-1 implementation began to become tangible and ceased to be a merely theoretical exercise, this groundwork proved to be invaluable. The co-creation of the AUP ensured that it was owned by multiple stakeholders, and not just by the few in charge of the implementation. This ownership helped to ensure that many colleagues and students became ambassadors for the 1-to-1 cause, effectively firefighting unfounded fears and misconceptions with facts and solutions to problems whilst at the same time reflecting on and learning from those fears and concerns which were well-founded and legitimate. This way we were able to convey our vision successfully to parents and the wider school community having considered and found solutions for the vast majority of the worries and concerns that they may have had regarding the 1-to-1 implementation.

Allaying the concerns of colleagues, students or parents about excessive screen-time or access to social networks, for example, was made much easier after having studied the perceived challenges and opportunities in careful detail.

However, it could be argued that, though one needs to ensure everyone is aware of the potential pitfalls, the best way to promote a 1-to-1 vision is to focus on the benefits it will bring to the daily business of teaching and learning. Once again, we can start by sampling student voice. Whenever we have asked our students about what they want from school, this is generally what they have said:

- Teachers with excellent subject knowledge
- Feedback that is delivered sensitively and effectively
- Resources that are media-rich and engaging

(Based on findings by Hattie and Yates)[6]

These student preferences are supported by findings of cognitive psychologists, such as Daniel Willingham, who highlights the importance of "conscious feedback"[7] and how technology can help present content to students in "inherently engaging" ways[8]. Once again, technology is available to lend a helping hand. However, despite such potential, the current prevalent discourse often presents technology in opposition to academic rigour, as if they were mutually incompatible and you had to have one or the other. This is nonsense and does not stand up to any form of serious scrutiny, as we hope to demonstrate later. For now, however, suffice to say that it is an obvious statement of fact that technology can facilitate the provision of feedback and help both students and teacher create engaging yet rigorous multimedia resources. But not everyone will be able to share this vision to begin with. If you are to successfully make a case for the use of mobile devices in your school and bring along as many people as

[6] Hattie, J. and Yates, G. (2014) Visible learning and the science of how we learn. Oxon: Routledge

[7] Willingham, D. (2009) Why don't students like school?. San Francisco: Jossey-Bass

[8] Willingham, D. (2010) Have technology and multitasking rewired how students learn?. American Educator, Summer 2010, pp. 23-28

possible, you will need to ensure that your strategy keeps sight of the most important tenet in this chapter: focus on using technology to support the processes involved in successful teaching and learning.

2.3.2 The value of 1-to-1 in extending learning beyond 3:30pm

But there is a whole other dimension to mobile technologies, in that they enable teaching and learning to take place more easily beyond the confines of the traditional school day. Many will insist in viewing this as an *alternative* to teaching and learning in school. It isn't. A good digital strategy would ensure that learning in school is extended and supported by the use of mobile technologies that enable students to continue learning beyond the school walls, acting as a link between formal and informal learning. Although face-to-face communication is often preferable, it is not always possible. We do not have to choose between *preferable* and *possible*, both are allowed.

The social aspect of the Internet has revolutionised the way we communicate. Access to mobile devices will inevitably contribute to the widening of opportunities to engage in online social activity. Hidden amongst all the sensationalist headlines decrying that we are alone in a sea of constant, inane chatter is the fact that we are writing, reading and communicating with each other on previously unprecedented scales. In fact, a recent study conducted in the United States showed that, despite all this technology - as the naysayers would have it - young people are actually more likely to have read a book (paper or digital) in the last twelve months than older adults[9]. The facts about the impact of digital technology in our lives run counter to the dystopian perceptions many adults hold about young people and their use of technology. Technology, as ever, presents us with both opportunities and challenges.

Opportunities because we can now use these communication tools to enable teachers to network and learn from others wherever they may be in the world in previously impossible ways; to support teachers in passing on

---

[9] http://www.pewInternet.org/2014/09/10/younger-americans-and-public-libraries/

their subject knowledge to learners; and to add a new dimension to the process of feeding back to enable learning to progress. But also challenges, as bullying and other kinds of already-existing inappropriate behaviour are released from the confines of the school corridors onto our social networks, which to this day remain vehemently a no-go area in most schools for this reason.

However, a problem has arisen when many schools have confused controlling access to communication technologies with total disengagement, thus depriving their students of models of appropriate behaviour, and often resulting in children who only have each other as role models. Paradoxically, we frequently accuse children of not behaving appropriately online when it was our job all along to educate them well. This problem is then compounded by the fact that many of the adults involved in education simply lack the experience and skills to be appropriate role models in the use of technology. This is why a greater, more concerted and more constructive involvement of schools in our digital lives is necessary if we want the best possible educational outcomes for our students.

Simply ignoring this other dimension of pupil behaviour seems to us to be grossly irresponsible. The use of mobile devices is becoming an ever more integral part of all our lives. Our pedagogy needs to takes stock of these social changes and explore ways in which teaching and learning can be supported by the appropriate use of technology, and in doing so ensuring that the processes of teaching and learning remain both relevant and familiar to our students without jeopardising educational rigour.

2.3.3 Conceptual models of technology use

So, does this mean technology is best used to support existing teaching and learning practices? No, it doesn't. When articulating a 1-to-1 vision it is important to highlight, not only how said vision will have a positive impact on existing practices, but also how it can act as a catalyst to help teachers and learners conceive ways to go about their business in ways which would have been previously impossible and which may result in more valuable educational outcomes. The work of Ruben Puentedura[10] helps to illustrate how technology can be used on a spectrum ranging from substitution to redefinition.

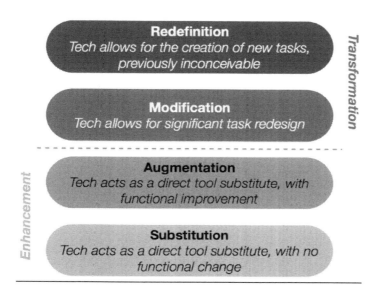

Puentedura establishes a clear distinction between mere enhancement and transformation in this 'SAMR' model. For him, the best use of technology stems from technology's potential to redefine tasks. In other words, using technology to continue doing what we have always done is less desirable than using technology to achieve that which had been previously impossible. Though tinkering around the edges can certainly bring moderate benefits, Puentedura's model suggests that the big educational gains will be achieved when we explore what we can do with technology that we couldn't do before.

For someone justifying the expense required to implement a 1-to-1 programme, it is therefore important to highlight, not only how tech can support existing practices, but also how it can help support teaching and learning in ways that are yet to be conceived. Puentedura's framework for technology adoption in schools therefore offers us a useful starting point to help paint a picture to students, teachers and the wider school community that illustrates how technology can act as a catalyst to transform teaching

---

10

http://www.hippasus.com/rrpweblog/archives/2014/06/29/LearningTechnology SAMRModel.pdf and learning practices for the better. However, crucially, this framework might also helps us understand when not to use technology. Whilst many view the SAMR model as a road map for technology integration, others find this interpretation unhelpful because it could be argued that any teacher who uses technology simply to substitute existing practices may not be using technology effectively. In fact, they may be using technology when they ought not to, when other methods are actually more effective.

In any case, conceptual models such as SAMR and Mishra and Koehler's Technological Pedagogical Content Knowledge framework (TPACK)[11] - about which we will talk in more detail in the next chapter - are essential points of reference for teachers seeking to understand how to successfully integrate technology use in schools.

2.3.4 A vision for mobile learning that supports your school's ethos

Whilst we have thus far emphasised the importance of focusing on pedagogy when making an educational case for the use of mobile devices, it would be erroneous to conclude that it ought to be the only focus, especially when articulating your vision to parents and the wider school community. We have already mentioned the role of intrinsic motivation and engagement, albeit with important caveats, but there are other factors that would need to be considered about the wider educational value of a 1-to-1 programme. Mapping the educational value that you think a 1-to-1 implementation might bring to your school's own values and ethos would be a good start. Below is an example of how Harrogate Grammar School has done this. The following extract is taken from their website[12]:

---

[11] http://www.matt-koehler.com/tpack/tpack-explained/
[12] http://www.harrogategrammar.co.uk/school/why/ipads-for-learning/ Retrieved 18.10.14

> **The** reasons for adopting the 1-1 iPad scheme were:
>
> - to ensure equality of access to the internet at school and at home
>
> - to prepare students for working and living in a digital age
>
> - to support self-led research and problem solving
>
> - to improve the quality of feedback, home learning and collaboration
>
> With the digital world developing so fast we are extremely proud of our students' and teachers' innovative use of technology to enhance the teaching & learning experience all students have. However, along with this and perhaps one of the most surprising benefits has been the shift in culture to one of a greater level of trust and respect.

The most important aspects of this particular school's ethos are excellence, enterprise, creativity, endeavour, considerate behaviour and respect. You can immediately see how these values are reflected and complemented by their statement of reasons to roll out a tablet implementation. Students, who are proud of their school, and parents, who are generally aligned to the school's ethos, will want to know and be reassured about how your proposals to allow children to use mobile devices compliment rather than run counter to the wider school aims to which they are already subscribed.

Finally, in making our educational case, we must consider the role of digital technology in today's world and how best to equip our students with the knowledge and skills necessary to effectively, responsibly, safely and critically navigate, evaluate and create digital artefacts using a range of digital technologies. This combination of knowledge and skills is commonly referred to as *digital literacy* and is an aspect of education that is often confined to infrequent PSHE sessions that by and large focus mainly on the negative aspects of technology use. A strategy to ensure that technology is used to further educational aims offers us the perfect opportunity to promote digital literacy as an essential aspect of what constitutes a good education for children today.

Section 2.4 Examining the evidence base for mobile learning

In recent years, the education sector has woken up to the need to make decisions which are informed by evidence of what works, and this culture of enquiry has gained momentum as budgets have been squeezed and schools' attitudes to innovative risk taking have changed.

This is a slightly backwards looking mindset ('we should do more of what we know worked in the past') which, when taken to the extremes that it sadly often is, negates the possibility of new things being even better. It discourages experimentation, labelling it wasteful and indulgent and, from a very high and snooty horse, pouring scorn on the efforts of innovative teachers trying to make things better with technology.

In the absence of any real, nuanced measure of 'learning', exam results are usually resorted to as a blunt proxy for educational impact. And as anyone who has spent any time doing Easter holiday intervention with Year 11 will tell you, exam results are not a very accurate measure of what a student has learned in their time at school. Yet the question most frequently asked of any educational technologist is 'how do you know it works? What's the impact?' and the only answer that will suffice is one with a number in it. But as any fool knows, not everything that counts can be counted. The attitude that dismisses an intervention as unevidenced just because it doesn't show up in GCSE English scores does a disservice to learners, who are more than the exams that they pass (or fail). This is, frankly, a lazy attitude to research.

What we need to do is to find proxy indicators that can be linked to general progress. Rather than trying to measure how technologies impact directly on outcomes, which is notoriously difficult to do convincingly, could we not instead measure how technologies impact on the daily business of teaching and learning? For example, how do technologies impact on the delivery of content, on the giving of feedback, on the quality of the homework? But this requires sustained effort. Often evidence is said to be found after laptops or tablets have been parachuted into a setting to see if magic happens. Unsurprisingly, however, magic doesn't tend to happen, which is why the evidence that is obtained from these studies has to be weighed up against that evidence that stems from schools that have successfully introduced and sustained a 1-to-1 environment and are able to provide evidence of how technology impacts on how technology supports the individual processes involved in teaching and learning.

From this perspective, context is crucial. It is not good enough to ask where the evidence is, what we need to ask is *what evidence is there for X in Y context?* When it comes to tablets, Wilma Clark and Rosemary Luckin from the Institute of Education, University of London, say this:

"The question we should be asked is not 'can iPads support learning?', but rather, 'how can iPads support collaborative learning, or exploratory learning', or whatever. The iPad is one of a range of tools that can help learning, and when it is used wisely it can be effective."[13]

It seems to me like those of us whose practice is impacted positively every single day by the judicious use of technology are forever feeling the need to qualify our experience by saying "when used wisely" or "when applied effectively". This is a rather bland statement of the obvious, as anything and everything can be used effectively or ineffectively, from pens to exercise books, from interactive whiteboards to the Internet. So, from now on, when we refer to the use of technology in schools, please assume that we mean technology that is used *effectively, wisely and judiciously*.

For a little more on this debate, please see Section 9.1 at the end of the book. For now, what you need to know is that no one knows anything for certain about the quantifiable effects of 1-to-1 learning, but that if you visit a school that has implemented it well, you will leave in no doubt as to the real impact mobile learning is having on students' day-to-day education. A good example of this is to be seen in one of the author's schools. Whilst Dan would be hard pushed to demonstrate that his 1-to-1 was the identifiable cause of the exam success of students at Stephen Perse Foundation, their recent inspection report[14] clearly identified its impact on learning.

---

[13] Clark, W. and Luckin, R. (2013) What the research says - iPads in the classroom. Institute of Education, University of London
[14] http://www.isi.net/schools/6777/

2.4.1 Emerging social research evidence

Much of the research that has looked into the efficacy of technology applied to instructional situations dates from before tablets became commonplace in wider society and has looked into the viability of computers as teaching and learning aid. According to Higgins et al. the focus has now changed from *"whether or not to use them in teaching and learning, to understanding which technologies can be used for what specific educational purposes and then to investigate how best they can be used and embedded across the range of educational contexts in schools"*.[15]

And when one looks for contexts where technology has been embedded, it is not difficult to find schools which attribute their academic improvement partly to the implementation of technology. When Rory Cellan-Jones, technology reporter for the BBC, visited the Essa Academy in Bolton, he felt the usual suspicion and scepticism with which new miracle cures or snake oils are, rightly, viewed. However, during his visit, he was shown how tablets had had a massive impact on several aspects of school life. Cellan-Jones wrote "photocopying expenses had plunged, with far fewer worksheets printed, and the cost of managing student behaviour was dramatically lower. With pupils more engaged, there had been a big improvement in their conduct at school."[16] When looking into the success of London schools, education writer Laura McInerney realised that it was due partly to technology and noted that "hidden technology was everywhere". McInerney believes that "London's successes didn't just come about 'because of collaboration' but because tools became available to make collaboration possible." [17] When looking at the US, it is frequent to see references to the Los Angeles Unified School District iPad fiasco[18], which, if anything, proves that little forethought and poor planning can indeed result in disaster. However, for every horror story there are many more examples of schools, such as the East Mooresville Intermediate School[19],

---

[15] Higgins, S., Xiao Z. and Katsipataki M. (2012) The impact of digital technology on learning. Durham University

[16] http://www.bbc.co.uk/news/technology-20667870

[17] http://www.lkmco.org/article/londons-schools-success-down-microsoft-and-mobile-phones-20072014

[18] http://larrycuban.wordpress.com/2013/12/06/a-second-look-at-ipads-in-los-angeles/

that explicitly associate academic success with successful implementation of mobile technology, despite the dearth of academic research into the subject. Surely any research ought to be looking into why these 1-to-1 implementations are successful, rather than simply focusing on why certain implementations fail.

Recent research carried out into whether digital technology could be useful to education has concluded that technology is beneficial and produces *"a low level of improvement"*. It also suggests that, perhaps unsurprisingly, *"it is not whether technology is used (or not) which makes the difference, but how well the technology is used to support teaching and learning"* (Higgins et al.[20]). As you can imagine, this is not good news really for someone trying to convince a bunch of financially constrained governors to throw money at mobile technology in the hope that it is appropriately used.

So, at first glance, it appears that what research there is on the use of digital technologies to support teaching and learning suggests that its impact is so close to neutral that it may not be a sound investment compared to other, more impactful interventions, and that the cost incurred in using the technology is much greater than the benefit received - this is a concept referred to in microeconomic theory as *opportunity cost*. The problem with this analysis, in our view, is that it assumes that technology is itself an intervention, rather than a mediator and facilitator of more impactful interventions, and that effective technology and good teaching are concepts that can be looked into separately, rather than flip sides of the same coin. Put simply, a lot of the stuff that's shown to work makes some use of technology to help it do so. These things aren't cleanly separable. The reasons for this are mainly down to measurability. We tend to bestow greater significance to that which we can easily measure, e.g. test results or grades, than to any value that may have been added by a particular intervention but is much harder to measure, e.g. fostering independence, resilience or creativity.

---

[19] http://www.nytimes.com/2012/02/13/education/mooresville-school-district-a-laptop-success-story.html
[20] Higgins, S., Xiao Z. and Katsipataki M. (2012) The impact of digital technology on learning. Durham University

2.4.2 Meta-studies and their limitations

This raises the question of whether technology use in schools can be measured as an intervention. The meta-studies available, chiefly those undertaken by Hattie and Yates, have generally looked at technology as an add-on to the classroom. That is to say, they've put computers (not tablets - some of the studies go back to the early nineties) in front of students in classrooms and tried to measure whether the learning outcomes improved as a result. Hattie and Yates found *"the impact of computers upon student achievement was found to be generally positive"*.[21] Computer-assisted instruction and instructional media were found to have overall effect sizes of 0.31 and 0.30 respectively (an effect size of 0.5 is roughly equivalent to a one grade leap at GCSE). Another example of measuring technology as an intervention comes from research undertaken by the Education Endowment Foundation, which also suggests moderate positive effects of +4 months (they estimated impact in terms of additional months progress you might expect pupils to make as a result of an approach being used in school). However, much more impressive effect sizes and impact are found in other strategies and interventions, mainly quality of teaching, learning to learn strategies and feedback.

So, in a sense, we are measuring technology against these and other important aspects of teaching and learning. No wonder then the impact on learning outcomes is often found to be slightly underwhelming. In reality, however, teachers do not stop giving feedback to use technology, or stop using technology to give feedback. Teachers do not stop teaching to use technology, nor do they stop using technology to start teaching. Technology is already woven into the fabric of schools. Teachers already employ digital technologies to plan and deliver lessons and feedback. Students already find technology an appealing, motivating and effective addition to their learning toolkit. The notion that technology can be measured as a separate intervention is therefore questionable, especially when you consider that the best, most effective use of technology in schools is when it supports the processes involved in teaching and learning, not when it runs parallel to them.

[21] Hattie, J. and Yates, G. (2014) Visible learning and the science of how we learn. Oxon: Routledge

2.4.3 Triangulation with other sources of evidence

When viewed from this wider perspective, one might ask what actually constitutes good evidence and whether, in education, professional judgement ought to, not only complement, but also temper what research suggests. Professor Biesta of the University of Luxembourg suggests that research is often limited to *"questions about the effectiveness of educational means and techniques, forgetting, among other things, that what counts as "effective" crucially depends on judgements about what is educationally desirable"*. He adds: *"judgement in education is not simply about what is possible (a factual judgement) but about what is educationally desirable (a value judgement)"*.[22] When applied to education, Professor Sandra Nutley of the University of St Andrews suggests that randomised controlled trials, the gold standard in medical research, if they are to be used in education more widely, need *"to be complemented by other forms of evidence, such as qualitative research and survey evidence if we want to know, not only how something works, but also whether it's right for this particular group of people"*. In her view *"many schemes only recognise practices and programmes that are underpinned by the strongest of evidence bases. This can stifle innovation, especially where funding is tied to the use of only recognised policies and programmes. There is merit in programmes that seek to recognise practices that may be helpful but do not yet have a strong evidence base to underpin them"*.[23] In other words, one should not stop exploring new opportunities simply because the evidence base is deemed to be insufficient, as it may still be developing.

Apple only launched the iPad, which has come to represent the watershed in school mobile learning schemes, in 2010 and, although some enlightening case studies have been compiled, the research and evidence base supporting the use of mobile devices in education is still thin on the ground, as you might expect from a technology that is only toddling its way into our schools. This, however, doesn't mean that there isn't any. Evidence of how the processes involved in teaching and learning can be supported by

---

[22] Biesta, G. (2007), Why "What works" won't work: Evidence-based practice and the democratic deficit in educational research. Educational Theory, 57: 1–22.
[23] http://vimeo.com/86105834

digital technologies is continually emerging. The views of leading academics in the field are reflected in Nesta's report *Decoding Learning*[24], which clearly shows how digital technology can support some of these processes:

- Learning from experts - Theories of learning emphasise the role of a more knowledgeable other, or expert, in guiding learners. This could be a peer, but is more usually a teacher. Nesta's research has found that digital technology offers new ways of presenting ideas, through animations, video lectures or podcasts.

- Learning with others - Research highlights three particularly promising areas for development: *representational* tools that enable the activities taking place to be presented to the learners; *scaffolding tools* that provide a structure for learning with others; and *communication* tools that support learners working at a distance from each other to collaborate.

- Learning through making - Digital technology can bring the idea of constructionism alive. Learners can construct anything in their imagination; and they can then share, discuss, reflect upon and, ultimately, to learn about that construction.

- Learning through exploring - Digital tools can provide new and engaging ways to explore information, and offer new ways to structure the environment that learners explore. The evidence in the few examples found was of a high quality and suggests that technology does offer the potential to enhance learning through exploration, an aspect which the authors of the report found to be currently underused and undervalued within educational settings.

- Learning through inquiry - Technology can be used to organise inquiry that might otherwise be difficult to accomplish, to change how learners look at problem solving, and to connect learners' inquiries to 'real world' scenarios.

- Learning through practising - The report found that the use of technology to support practice is rarely seen to be innovative; but promising developments include the use of rich multimodal

---

[24] Luckin, R., Bligh, B., Manches, A., Ainsworth, S., Crook, C. and Noss, R. (2012) Decoding Learning: The proof, promise and potential of digital education. London: Nesta.

environments that can create challenging problems and provide appropriate feedback.

- Learning from assessment - The report also highlighted digital technologies' potential to support formative assessment or the assessment of other skills. It found that using social networks and read-write technologies, such as web 2.0, can facilitate peer, collaborative and self-guided learning. Combining data, captured through a variety of digital tools, with learning analytics was found to offer great promise for assessment.

- Learning in and across settings - Finally, Nesta's research suggested that technology can help learners apply and transfer learning from one setting, such as a lesson at school, to another, such as a field trip or the home.

(Source: Nesta's Decoding Learning Report[25])

Section 2.5 What are the advantages and disadvantages of the different models?

As the overarching question facing school leaders shifts from whether to use mobile devices to how to manage and encourage their use to support teaching and learning objectives, schools have begun to experiment with ways and means to ensure that all of their pupils (or at least as many as possible) have access to mobile devices during their schooling. The two most commonly used approaches are Bring Your Own Device (BYOD) and 1-to-1, which differ mainly in the means by which the devices are acquired and the extent to which they can be successfully integrated into learning. As the name implies, BYOD encourages students to bring devices that they already own. Some schools apply a BYOD philosophy that states students can bring their own device, whilst others state that students must bring their own device. This subtle difference will have repercussions that we will look into below. On the other hand, in a 1-to-1 environment the school has decided which device students ought to be using and puts in place the means by which students can acquire it.

---

[25] http://www.nesta.org.uk/publications/decoding-learning

Both systems have been shown to work with differing degrees of success and the decision about which system your school ultimately opts for will have to be made after careful consideration of that particular school's circumstances. Most importantly, both systems will require strong leadership and good infrastructures. Clearly there is not a one-size-fits-all model and school leaders must weigh up carefully the different pros and cons of each approach. Overleaf is a table that might help you in your decision:

BYOD Positives

- Harnesses the technology that students already have

- Cheaper option for schools (although reliable wi-fi infrastructure is still required)

- School involvement in managing devices is low to non-existent

- Initial findings suggest students prefer this option

1 to 1 Positives

- Uniformity of device, applications and processes and a consequently richer tool set

- Single device and operating system allows teachers to plan 'higher order' activities with confidence

- Training can be provided to teachers more effectively and good practice is more easily spread

- Raises the bar and introduces expectation of usage

- Facilitates control of device content through mobile device management software

- Schools can more easily facilitate access to their networked systems and drives

- Full integration with classroom AV brings new opportunities and lesson cultures

- Instances of inappropriate use or behaviour can be policed more easily

- All these factors may contribute to more consistent use in lessons and, therefore, change is more likely to take place and to be sustained, resulting in a greater likelihood of improved learning outcomes

BYOD Negatives

- Brings the 'digital tools' standard down to the lowest common denominator; research and presentation tasks predominate as a result

- A mixed economy where there is a multitude of applications and operating systems is harder for teachers to plan for

- Requires more teacher expertise and confidence

- Passively embraced by teachers, if at all, and therefore unlikely to lead to much change

- Access to schools' networked systems and drives is problematic

- Might exacerbate inequality

- Instances of inappropriate use of behaviours are harder to police

- Legitimises the use of mobile phones in lessons, which may just provide cover for disruptive and off-task behaviour

- Poor integration with classroom AV

- All these factors may contribute to less consistent use in lessons and may cause teachers to fear similar attempts to use technology positively in the future

1 to 1 Negatives

- Financially expensive

- Management overhead, as the school is, in varying degrees, managing the devices

- Staff development overhead, as all teachers will need to be trained to be able to take advantage of this technology whenever it adds value?

Whilst BYOD is attractive because it makes the most of the tools students are already using and is a cheaper option from the outset, schools must weigh up any potential positive impact mobile devices might bring against all the other considerations. Schools tend to prefer the uniformity provided by a single operating system and device, the ability to determine which device staff and students will use and the inherent benefits of staff/ student training provision and device management. Having said this, often the decisive factor for schools facing this particular fork in the road is not what is pedagogically desirable but rather what is financially affordable. In other words, although a 1-to-1 model might be most attractive and beneficial to schools, the huge expense it entails often puts it beyond the reach of most school budgets.

So, if expense is what usually puts the brakes on mobile device initiatives, it might help to consider what expensive means. There is clearly the financial expense. In these terms the cost of an 1-to-1 initiative for the average secondary school will be somewhere between £150,000 and £200,000 per annum, plus the cost of infrastructure, which we will look into in more detail later on. This is before any other IT costs - such as network maintenance, Wi-Fi infrastructure or consumables - are taken into account. It is clearly a huge sum of money for any budget. This is why schools often resort to parental contributions of around £5 to £20 per month to finance these initiatives. We will explore ways in which these initiatives can be financed in Chapter 4.

However, the pill can be sweetened substantially by analysing carefully what other financial expenses the school incurs and offsetting them against the longer term of a mobile device implementation. For example, if your school spends £5,000 to £10,000 yearly on printers, printing consumables, paper and photocopying, might the ubiquity of mobile devices around school reduce the need for printing and photocopying thus resulting in substantial savings in the medium to long term? Similarly large savings can derive from the fact that essentially students will be carrying with them most - if not all - their computing needs. School leaders can then justify the re-routing of funds that would have been otherwise used to replace or purchase desktop computers to a 1-to-1 programme. Clearly, We are not suggesting that these savings can offset the cost of a 1-to-1 initiative in its totality, but looking to the long term might help to mitigate some of the financial concerns associated with mobile device implementation.

But expensive can be measured in other ways as well. Take the example of the academy with a specialism in technology and an ethos that encourages digital literacy and other skills that are commonly referred to as '21st century skills'. Take also the case of the independent school that seeks to establish itself apart from fierce local competition through a clear focus on improving teaching and learning practices and processes linked to the implementation of a 1-to-1 programme in order to attract demanding, technologically-aware middle-class parents. Both will have to consider financial expense against the cost of non-implementation. Perversely, for some schools, the most expensive option in the long run might turn out be to avoid a mobile device implementation.

Nevertheless, given the alternatives available to schools currently and after careful analysis of both the opportunities and challenges, the authors of this book unanimously agree that a 1-to-1 model offers the best option to schools who seek to retain control over how the technology can be used and implemented. Whilst BYOD can seem very attractive due to the low financial cost, key factors such as uniformity of device and integration with the schools existing systems mean that, at the time of writing, a 1-to-1 environment is much more likely to succeed.

However, a final consideration must be given to technology's capacity to change the rules of the game with single, unexpected, decisive strokes. For instance, it is possible to imagine a time in the near future in which all apps and operating systems are browser based. This is already the path down which Google is travelling with Google Apps and Chrome, for example. It is perfectly conceivable that, not too long from now, agonising over which device is best is a thing of the past, as all students will need is a device with access to the Internet. In October 2014, Google announced a key milestone on this route - the availability of Adobe's Photoshop for Chromebook. BYOD clearly becomes a more attractive option in this scenario. Whatever your school decides - whether it's BYOD, 1-to-1 or non-implementation - will have to be based on your specific needs and circumstances. As we have already said in this chapter, context is everything and, although lessons can be learnt, what works really well in one setting does not necessarily work well in others.

3 PLANNING & PREPARING

Section 3.1 Staffing structures to ensure embedded change

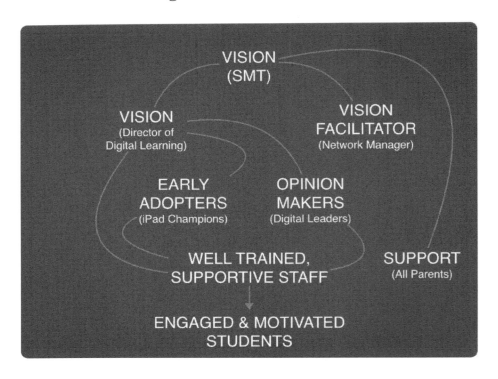

3.1.1Head's vision & buy-in

Change within a school is often a rare and precious thing. Successful, sustained change even more so. Rightly or wrongly, embedded and long-lasting change will only come to a school where the Headteacher is on board with the project. This has never been truer than with the integration of new technology.

In an ideal world, the Head of the school will be the one suggesting and driving this change forward with a clear understanding of what it is they want to achieve and the timeframe for this. If this is not the case, then the next best scenario is for the Head to be sympathetic to the cause and see its merits. If your school does not fall into one of these two categories then the integration of mobile technology will be fraught with challenge and may ultimately fail.

Embedding technology across the curriculum via the use of mobile devices is expensive and challenging. When it is done with the right people in place it can be revolutionary and inspiring, when this is not the case, you can end up with a lot of technology sitting in boxes, losing its investors a lot of money and ultimately, credibility.

The problem for a Headteacher is knowing what the vision should look like. It's all too easy to be invited to someone else's shiny new-build academy that has retracting walls, bean bags instead of desks, a library with more computers than books, every student carrying around an iPad, and believe that this is the future, but not if you can't have the new building to go with it. You can borrow ideas, but you can't borrow situations. It's worth considering that nothing works everywhere, and everything works somewhere.

Equally difficult is the question of whether or not an iPad or any other mobile device is going to increase your grades in public exams, because let's face it, that matters to Headteachers as much as anything, especially when funding is on the line.

So let's address these concerns...

Newly built schools are certainly designed for a new era of teaching and learning, but this new era is yet to be defined and certainly if mobile learning's success is defined by a building, then hasn't something gone horribly wrong? What is most useful about a newly built school is infrastructure; things like wireless Internet wherever you walk - something that any school can have. A building does not create success, the people that inhabit it do. Yes, it is easier to 'start over' if you have a new school to move into, but the beauty of this project, is that it is akin to such a thing; the introduction of mobile technology can rebuild a school's whole attitude to teaching and learning if that is your vision.

Conversely, that vision may be too extreme, and indeed, we think often this is an unhelpful starting point. The reality of mobile technology is that it is a new tool. It doesn't have to mean a completely fresh start; it often absolutely *shouldn't* mean this! So many great things will already be happening in your schools, why would you want to throw that out because of a new tool? Not many people thought that the move from chalkboard to whiteboard to interactive whiteboard was going to completely rewrite education and indeed these tools have not. Good teaching and good learning prevail and the people that take ownership of their practices as teachers will utilise the resources they are given in the best possible way.

An iPad (or any other zeitgeist-capturing slab of glass and tin) is a tool. It can do great things; it can do things that have not been possible before. But not everything you do needs to be new.

There are a number of stories about schools that have radically improved their exam results and attribute this exclusively to iPads. Whilst there may be some loose correlation, it is unlikely that this is an unassailable and accepted truth. Often these stories take place in deprived areas and there are other agents of change shaping the path of the school at the same time. Thus far, evidence of mobile devices improving academic outcomes is largely anecdotal (see the section on Evidence at the end of the book for more detail). We absolutely believe that as time goes by and studies are given enough time to analyse data over significant periods of time, we will discover that evidence of technology's contribution to the improvement of academic outcomes will build up and become clearer. Although a very different context and in pursuit of different outcomes, one only needs to look at the work of Sugata Mitra's 'Hole in the Wall' research to know that technology can empower and educate without adult interference.

Nonetheless, one cannot expect a Head to buy-in to a project based on possible outcomes and success stories from around the globe that don't necessarily translate to their own context, or address their specific challenges. We think there is a far more plausible and healthy level at which to buy-in to the idea that technology needs to be embedded across a school; it already is. Ubiquitous Internet access and mobile device ownership amongst students are at their highest levels yet, and this will only increase. In 2010 Mary Meeker, the head of Morgan Stanley's global technology research team, predicted that 2014 would be the year that mobile Internet users would surpass desktop Internet users.[26] Now, 2015 is believed to be the year when tablet sales alone, will surpass that of PCs.[27] Virtual Reality headsets are an actual reality. The number of active users on Facebook is more than three times the population of the USA. Technology is everywhere. It is in our schools and we believe that a lot of time and energy has gone into overlooking, ignoring or trying to lock down this technology. Headteachers need to be prepared to engage with technology and to harness its almost limitless potential for teaching and learning.

Technology may or may not actively make students more intelligent or effective, but technology is playing and will continue to play an increasingly significant part in their lives. The role of a school is to educate the whole person, and a big part of this is ensuring that young people understand the benefits and dangers of the world in which they live and the technology they carry around with them, and it is also to prepare them for life after school. It seems increasingly unlikely that our young people will go on to do jobs that tether them to a desktop computer. Indeed the jobs that they go on to do possibly don't exist yet and if they do, there seems little doubt that over the next few years technology will play its part in redefining these roles.

---

[26] https://gigaom.com/2010/04/12/mary-meeker-mobile-Internet-will-soon-overtake-fixed-Internet/
[27] http://www.extremetech.com/computing/185937-in-2015-tablet-sales-will-finally-surpass-pcs-fulfilling-steve-jobs-post-pc-prophecy

Schools have always reflected in microcosm the societies they exist in and it is the fundamental duty of education to prepare people for useful lives. It doesn't seem credible that a successful school can ignore the advantages and inescapability of mobile learning.

Once a Headteacher has taken the decision to explore the possibilities of technology within their school, they then need to surround themselves with people who will assist them in making good, clear and future-proof decisions about how best to implement this exciting change.

3.1.2 The importance of strategic leadership, not just the Head's vision

The Director of Innovation/ Technology role

A Headteacher cannot be expected to become an expert in every subject taught in their school and so it is true with overseeing the integration of technology into a school; they may have the vision, but they certainly won't be able to devote the amount of time needed to make such a complex project succeed on the ground.

What is essential however, is that they have a clear idea of who they need to oversee this project.

Drawing up a job description is a complex part of this process. The role is still relatively new and frankly there is a limited supply of people who could fill it effectively.

The first challenge is what to call it. Director/ Head/ Leader of…

- eLearning?
- Digital Strategy?
- Technology?

The reality is that this does not matter, so long as the school and the incumbent are clear about what the role means within their context. What is hopefully obvious, is that the role has little to do with the curriculum subjects of ICT or Computer Science and would not benefit from being encouraged to manage a Head of Department job with what ultimately is a senior management role (more of this later). Indeed the people that have most successfully embodied this role to date have no formal training in ICT; they are teachers who have passionately advocated the use of technology for the benefits of teaching and learning. Adam is an English teacher, José MFL, Dan PE and Dominic History. For the sake of clarity, We will refer to this job as Director of Technology throughout the remainder of this section.

The skill-set is fairly obvious in one sense, but also highly demanding. It will be challenging to fulfil all of the criteria laid out below, so the aim of this section is to flesh out what are the key areas of the job and the things that simply cannot be compromised.

Key Requirements for a Director of Technology role:

- A relentless focus on learning;
- It should encompass the use of technology across every aspect of school-life;
- It should be part of the School Leadership Team;
- The focus should be on supporting staff development;
- It should line-manage the school's technical staff as they're the ones who'll operationalise the strategy.

Skills:

- Listening – understanding and integrating the needs of students & their learning into the school's approach to technology use;
- Visioning – understanding what emerging technologies make possible, and working out if they could contribute to the school's educational aims;
- Strategising – planning how the vision is to be delivered and the when/ what/ where/ who and how of making it come to life;
- Coaching – supporting classroom staff in the confident and effective use of technology for learning;

- Training – designing and delivering a program of CPD aligned to the strategy;
- Mentoring – developing additional capacity within the school, encouraging subject champions to become engines of change within their departments;
- Liaising – feeding in the expertise and expectations of the school's governance and wider community of parents, employers and other education professionals;
- Reflecting – learning from others in similar roles around the world.

The individual should be:

- A great teacher with a passion for their chosen career and strong experience of applying technology to enhance teaching and learning;
- Broadly aware of the use of technology across a school;
- Commercially savvy; able to manage a complex combination of suppliers, projects and contracts;
- Emotionally mature and empathetic, with a foot in both camps so that they are able to translate & mediate between teachers and technical staff;
- A skilled trainer, with great communication skills and educational credibility, who is able to demystify technology and reveal its relevance;
- A persistent and optimistic character, who can demonstrate determination in the face of setbacks;
- Inquisitive and inventive enough to stay abreast of developments and spot opportunities to innovate and, equally, find practical solutions to teaching or technical problems;
- Able to monitor and assess both formally and informally the needs of colleagues and pupils, and to respond to them;
- Eternally grounded in what we know about effective learning and teaching, with the skepticism required to apply technology only where it accelerates, deepens, adds value or makes the previously impossible possible.

This role definitely represents a significant investment by a school in the development of technology, but without it, money spent on technology itself is likely to result in limited impact.

You could treat the above list as a job description for the ideal Director of Technology. Reality dictates that as with anything of this sort, compromises must be made. So the thing to know in advance is what you cannot live without and as this role is so new, that can be difficult to understand at the outset.

We believe it is utterly essential that the person filling this role is a teacher. Preferably a teacher with some years of experience and one who has a strong reputation for delivering teaching of a high standard. The reason for this is two-fold:

- You will end up with a Director of Technology who has as much credibility amongst the teachers as they do what the rest of the faculty do and can genuinely empathise with staff when they say that there is not enough time, or resources, or that they are frustrated at having to learn a new way of doing things. This means that the Director of Technology will be likely only to propose changes and initiatives that he/ she really does believe in and knows are effective in the classroom. We spent much of our early years in similar posts trying out new ideas either at home or with small groups of students so that we delivered tried and tested, legitimate improvements to the way things were being done already;
- They are more likely to be in a position to recognise where change is possible and necessary and should more easily find themselves able to step up to the TPACK model[28] and negotiate what is a complex relationship as both teacher and trainer.

The TPACK model (shown below) is a development of an earlier theory by Lee Shulman in 1986, that described what made an effective teacher. This

---

[28] Mishra, P., & Koehler, M. J. (2006). Technological Pedagogical Content Knowledge: A new framework for teacher knowledge. *Teachers College Record. 108*(6), 1017-1054.

new model incorporates technology into the mix and gives simple but useful framework against which to examine what you want from your teachers and who is best placed to guide them to this point.

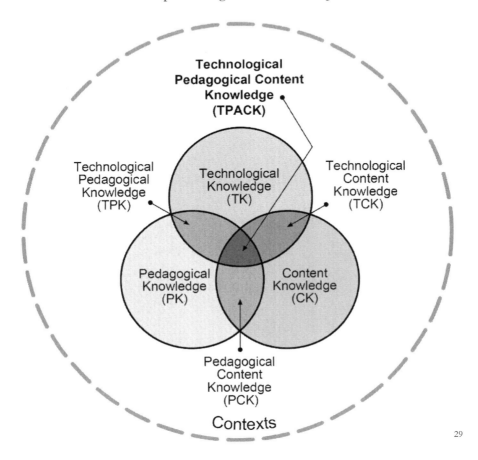

It is assumed that a good teacher falls into the 'PCK' area of the diagram - that is, they know their subject and they also know how to go about teaching. Using this diagram, it is easy to understand that your Director of Technology should fall into the red area in the centre. This supports the idea that they need to be an excellent teacher first and foremost as to fulfil this model's criteria of being able to integrate technology into teaching and learning, one must have a strong grasp on both pedagogical practice and

---

[29] http://tpack.org

one's own subject knowledge, as well as a clear grasp of how technology can interact with these two areas simultaneously. One can also see therefore, that the Director of Technology cannot fall into the red zone for subjects outside their own, but rather need to occupy the 'PTK' zone and pull teachers who are in the 'TCK' zone into the red area through outstanding training and advice.

So on one level the Director of Technology is an example to hold up to others; someone of whom a Headteacher can say 'this is how it's done.' It should also be clear that it is not possible for the Director of Technology to be able to confidently find him/herself in the red zone with every teacher they talk to if they are not discussing their own subject. Indeed the real skill of the Director of Technology role is to find someone who places themself in the upper right section of this diagram - someone who understand Pedagogy and Technology and their intrinsic relationship. If you have the right person, then they will be able to use their understanding of this combination and take those who are already strong practitioners (i.e. those who are in the upper right area combining Content and Pedagogy) and draw them in towards the centre through strong training and coaching.

The other key attribute that you can't do without is that the role is taken on by someone who has a clear vision that coincides with a sound understanding or technology. That said, all of the decisions made will once again be predetermined by the fact that your DoT role is all about teaching and learning.

Irrespective of whether the Headteacher is a technology enthusiast or not, key decisions will be made or at least significantly influenced by the vision of the Director of Technology. Not every person who does this job needs to have the same vision and there is not a right way of doing things. However, there are obvious things that you would expect this person to have considered:

- Why are we making the move to mobile learning in THIS school?
- What is the right device for THIS school?
- What is the right timeframe for deployment for THIS school?
- What will good teaching and learning look like with a mobile device?
- Who from the staff are likely to champion this process?

- Who from the staff are likely to need the most encouragement or are likely to try to block this change?
- Is the infrastructure of the school ready to support this change?
- Is the technical support team right for this change?
- How can we involve the students in the process as early as possible?
- How will we measure the success of this project at various points in time?
- Beyond the device, what other changes will be introduced because of this initiative (i.e. cloud-based software, support for students with learning difficulties, the way exams are sat)?
- How will I engage with and get support from subject leaders?
- How will I engage with and get support from pastoral leaders?

These are all big questions, but they are ones the Director of Technology will need to constantly juggle, on top of the seemingly endless smaller questions that seem to take up an unprecedented amount of time (the make and colour of the device case being one such example!).

It is because of the depth and range of skills required from this role that it makes sense for it to be carried out by a senior leader. This person needs to be able to dedicate significant time to the project, to have status with staff, students and other key stakeholders like governors and parents if the vision is to be carried through. And, crucially, needs a seat at the top table so that they are best able to ensure that everyone is behind the effort and that resources (particularly CPD time) will be forthcoming.

This role is unique in many ways and requires a delicate balance of skills. It should not be a job that is tacked onto another existing one. A Head of Department could not perform this role effectively, nor could a teacher who has a full teaching timetable. Adam, Daniel and José currently work with an approximately 50% timetable and this gives them time to plan, implement, train and troubleshoot, but even this stretches their ability to observe and play a part in as many lessons as desirable. In teaching there is never enough time, but with a role like this it is important that the person leading has the opportunity to plan, implement and reflect in ways that will ensure mistakes are kept to a minimum and support is available for them to receive and give in equal measure. Ultimately your school is on the cusp of spending half a million pounds (see the section on Finance if that figure sounds fantastical!) and the most important part of that process is ensuring that you have the right people in the right place and a big part of that is ensuring that the leadership team has the expertise to guide the rest of the school through this new experience.

3.1.3   On-message technical support team

Not much happens in a school these days without IT support making it so. It's also fair to say that there are probably few people less appreciated within a school than the technical support personnel. They are invisible until something goes wrong and then if your printer isn't fixed fast enough, or the Wi-Fi goes down for a few hours, panic-driven, apocalyptic hysteria ensues and everything around you begins to crumble whilst you're on your knees sending another passive-aggressive email, begging for help - at least that's what we've heard.

This version of technical support (whether real or perceived) cannot be the one allowed to exist in your school if you are interested in embedding mobile learning across the curriculum.

It can often seem as though good IT support is hard to come by, but perhaps the truth is more that technicians with up to date, focused training are hard to come by. This may be because either they or the institution they are a part of do not see the need for such training, but it is as big a part of the overall needs for strong infrastructure as anything else.

Not all IT technicians and Network Managers will have the time or perhaps the get-up-and-go to seek out the answers to problems (and there will be many) along the way. This can be for a combination of reasons, but most likely it is because they haven't been engaged with and included in the discussions that have led to the point of executing the project.
Often one hears reports of 'old school' Network Managers who have locked down a school network as tightly as possible to keep it secure. Indeed that is how Network Managers have been trained and so it follows

that often, this is how they like to do their job. Their job is largely about the management of risk; it's natural for them to try and avoid it. So when you suddenly turn around to this person, (and lets not forget that this is a person who genuinely feels a real weight upon their shoulders in terms of the responsibility of keeping the network up and running without fault or delay) and you say let's start using Dropbox, and Gmail instead of Microsoft Exchange, and by the way we're introducing 900 mobile devices onto the network in September, it's not hugely surprising that the reaction isn't one of fist-pumping rejoicing.

It takes time to prepare a school to move towards a 1-to-1 mobile environment. The time is needed for both technical and psychological reasons. So much change can happen; buildings and people need to evolve and adapt. Never is this truer and almost simultaneously so, than for the technical support personnel in your school.

Without wishing to disparage the profession, it's also true to say that there are some technical staff who seem almost ideologically opposed to the use of Apple hardware, due to its proprietary nature and, let's be honest, the fact that it tends to work without the need for technical support… Mobile learning can be perceived as a threat, undermining a traditional power base. Unfortunately, technical staff can sometimes be in opposition to 1-to-1 plans, even though their role is to enable and deliver the school's technology vision.

However, to find a Network Manager who 'gets' mobile learning will become increasingly easy because a new wave of such people will be starting their careers in workplaces that have already made that change. but until that point, one cannot expect to simply find one that will completely buy in to your project unless you include them, talk to them, guide them and reassure them that the project has been thought through, that their job is safe so long as they are willing to adapt and that their opinions are valued.

If they are still unwilling to get 'on-message' then that is a different thing; it may be that you simply don't have the level of compatibility necessary to meet your needs. Often this resistance comes from having not quite adapted to a new world order; once upon a time, a Network Manager was a one-eyed king in the land of the blind; he knew every inch of his network and could control it with puppetmaster-like precision and now individual users are being empowered by 19 year old super-coders from Cupertino who want everyone to be an administrator of their own account. This is a difficult transition to make, however, in all likelihood, your Network Manager will be able to cope with and engage with this change, so long as you keep them in the loop and explain to him that this is a great opportunity for change and development rather than a way of making his skillset redundant.

If you win over the Network Manager and work in partnership with that person, then they will win over the rest of the technical support team, they will be able to show you where the strengths and weaknesses of that team lie and they will be able to help re-train or rebuild that team so that you have the right people doing the right jobs for you.

It's easy for a technical support team to become anxious about the change to mobile learning, especially if the chosen platform is not a Windows one. However, part of the process of helping them with this change is reassurance that many things are not changing, or at least not drastically, and indeed much of what they already do is simply becoming more important and more high profile. Network security for example, is close to the heart of most IT personnel (and is often a major cause for concern when discussing mobile learning) and this is an area that can be given renewed attention which should be seen as an exciting challenge. Similarly, there is a great chance to marry together systems that don't necessarily fit in an obvious way. Technicians who work through the process of getting Apple, Android or Chrome devices to work in tandem with a Windows network (which is what so many technicians are going to be asked to do), will be in demand and will be increasing their employment opportunities. And, there are so many options to explore in this arena, whether it be accessing Windows documents on an iPad, or syncing Active Directory credentials to work on a mobile device. Each success should both open the team up to the feeling that the change is becoming increasingly achievable and indeed, the right decision for the school.

What will be most effective in your school will be a matter or the specific personnel and the model of management you have chosen to follow based on what has already been discussed in this chapter. However, whatever the specifics, the Director of Technology and the Network Manager need to be compatible and to absolutely share the same goals and vision.

If one is to line manage the other then in reality the Director of Technology should be in the leading role as when all is said and done. The person who thinks first about teaching and learning and second about how and if a goal is possible, is the person who will drive through change more effectively. This arrangement ensures that technical decisions are always made in the light of the driving educational vision. The dog should wag the tail, if that's not too dismissive a metaphor.

We do also believe however, that the two roles can be a genuine partnership. The skill sets of these two people are simultaneously similar and different. One may understand where the other is coming from but both will ultimately be outsiders in the other's realm.

From a Headteacher's point of view, the right Network Manager needs to be a high-priority target. The project simply cannot progress if this person is not in place and helping drive forward the necessary changes at a technical level. What is also important is to appreciate that the job you're asking of your Network Manager and their team is not an inexpensive one. Not only should you be prepared to pay a premium for someone who already has the expertise to carry out your project but there needs to be a willingness to set aside funds for training and of course the changes to infrastructure which will be discussed elsewhere in this book. Whilst it all adds up in the short term, the investment means that the project is much more likely to succeed and most importantly, to stand the test of time.

An outstanding Network Manager will invariably be an unsung hero; a facilitator in every sense. Someone who manages their own staff effectively, sees where training and development are needed, understands what a modern, robust network looks like, can communicate effectively with teaching and support staff with a clear vision and 'human' vocabulary. Most importantly, an outstanding Network Manager will work with the

Headteacher and the Director of Technology and ensure that no one else ever knew how much change happened behind the scenes to ensure that when mobile learning began in earnest, it felt like it had always been possible.

3.1.4   Content creation role(s)

There is a fascinating new role emerging in schools that are progressing with their 1-to-1 mobile learning projects, a role that crosses over a multitude of different skills and areas within a school. It's a job for a person who is part technician, part teaching assistant, part teacher, part admin support, part creative genius.

It is a role that is in its early stages of definition and as yet, has not been set in stone because of the fast pace of change in this arena. In one of the author's schools, this role is defined as 'Digital Learning Technician', elsewhere they are known as a Digital Education Officer; even across these examples the role takes on significantly different guises. What is common to them is that this role is a necessary part of supporting the progress and success of the mobile learning project your school undertakes, by taking off some of the pressure of course creation and resourcing teachers through this time of change.

The role exists in very few schools and is difficult to fill because there simply isn't enough precedent for recruitment companies, or even potential candidates reading the TES jobs section to know who is the right fit for the job. Current post-holders have often been serendipitous finds, usually in other roles in the school.

Our experience of training teachers to prepare for this change is that a significant degree of anxiety comes from the idea that they have to rewrite or recreate or worse yet, start from scratch, with all of the resources they have been using up to this point.
Perhaps to some extent there is a nugget of truth in this. To best engage with this exciting opportunity we should all be given the time to review the folders of resources (digital or physical) that we carry around with us from

year to year, and take the time to edit, filter, delete and redesign what we had thought were cutting edge teaching materials (or at least steady and reliable staples).

The reality is that there is simply not time for that.
What needs to happen instead, is a three-pronged attack to ensure that teachers are ready to approach mobile learning within their classrooms positively.

Prong 1: Know where to find the easy-win resource.

One of the great advantages of this new-fangled technology drive is that there are hundreds of incredible resources being made available for teachers online. They simply need to know where to look and have someone on hand to keep them updated. Better still, they need someone to test drive apps and web resources so they only get fed quality content.

Prong 2: If in doubt, default to PDF

Many tablets, including the iPad, support the use of PDF in almost any app that generates content from Pages to Explain Everything. PDFs are everywhere and can be used in so many ways. Many resources reside in shared school drives as either PDFs or Word and PowerPoint files that can easily be turned into this file type. Whilst the result is not necessarily as impactful as creating an eBook, generating resources in PDF form and uploading them to some sort of curriculum delivery system is a great way of circulating tried and tested resources in a way that students can work with.

Prong 3: Pick one or two core resources and give them the full technological makeover

To really engage your staff in this journey it is best not to overwhelm them with information or set expectations so high that they revolt. Instead, it is good practice to encourage them to focus on just one or two resources that, if transformed effectively, will reap reward for them as well as giving them confidence and credibility in the classroom. This may be turning one module or one small scheme of work into a new interactive format, or recording a series of 5 or 6 short videos to kickstart a 'flipped learning' approach. Certainly if you follow later guidelines about staggering the start to your 1-to-1 program, you will find that this approach works incredibly well.

Each of these approaches is enhanced and simplified by having the right support personnel in place. It would be possible and perhaps even preferable to delegate each of these jobs to one individual who takes on board the sole responsibility for resources creation. This model is being successfully implemented in some schools and certainly alleviates pressure from teachers. It also means that there is a controllable uniformity for the way in which resources are created, giving a consistent student experience and a definite marketing angle for the school. The person employed into this incarnation of the role need not be full time and does not have to be highly skilled technically once they have been trained up to create resources in 'house style'.

The downside to formulating the role in this way is that it misses the opportunity of creating a role that supports the Director of Technology and offers a secondary intermediary between teachers and technical support.

Whilst more complex, our preference is for this role to be fulfilled by a person familiar with the technology being utilised (iPads for example) in a professional environment (say, Apple retail), but for this person to also be willing and able to work closely with students and teachers on problem-solving and content creation projects. This support person may be invited into a lesson to observe, to support technically, to offer feedback and advice on the way technology was being utilised in a way that the Director of Technology may also do.

The other issue with having someone in a content creation role rather than the role outlined above, is that there is a lack of ownership for teachers. The support technician who helps the Director of Technology train teachers how to use iTunes U and iBooks Author will be of more use to the academic staff in the long run and will more successfully embed technology across the curriculum in our opinion. If teachers do not actually create the resources they teach with, the level of personalized learning (one of the greatest potential benefits of a 1-to-1 project) is diminished.

This role could be a term-time only job, which would work well if the job was strictly limited to content creation. It could also work if the role was taken on by a part-time teacher or someone returning to work. However, if the person in the role has a more technical understanding than pure creation, as we outline above, you may find that this person can usefully be employed as an additional member of the IT support team during crucial maintenance periods which often fall in the school holidays. Nonetheless, like other 'term time, school hours' jobs, this position could be extremely attractive to your parent body. The right skill set may well be already at the school gates.

Whatever the model a school opts for, one thing is very clear; this role needs to exist so that there is an adequate support network for both the academic staff as a whole, but also the Director of Technology and technical support staff.

Section 3.2 A timeline for success

3.2.1 Piloting

The pilot phase of this project is probably one of the most important and yet over-looked stages of the process of mobile technology integration. Many schools launch headfirst into rollout schemes (of which, more later) and seem to adopt a sort of 'sink or swim' mentality to the whole thing, which given the level of investment is quite astonishing.

The point of a pilot is to test the concept in a low-risk environment. It is perfectly possible that your pilot will demonstrate that 1-to-1 isn't right for your school - and that's good, if it's an accurate conclusion. After all, the pilot stage isn't simply a political hoop-jump, you should actively be trying to understand if and then how you should do this.
Pilot schemes can in themselves vary dramatically depending on the school's appetite for risk, the financial and the time resource available. The starting point could be considering which device to use and therefore

involves buying or borrowing a range of devices on a very small scale and working out which one might work in a classroom. This is a challenging thing to do if there are multiple individuals involved in the decision-making process because undoubtedly people will disagree and favour devices for a variety of different reasons (such as how long they have to test it, how similar it is to what they already know, what their own idea of the right device is). It is far more simple if one or two people are the decision-makers and there is a clear set of criteria and ideas that need to be fulfilled; this returns us to the job description of the Director of Technology and his/her ability to have a clear vision and to get others on board. Also, though every school wants to go through this themselves, everyone else already has - the intelligence about which current device is right, right now, is out there without the need for pointless trials of the latest third-party, underpowered Windows 8 tablet.

If we move a step on from choosing a device, then the scale of a pilot is the next decision. Yet again, we are restricted by budgetary concerns, but arguably a pilot that does not facilitate a 1-to-1 environment in some way (unless this is not your final goal) would seem to be rather detrimental to the process. A situation where some do and some don't have a device in a class produces a very false set of results, always negative for the device, because all that is discovered is that those without can't do what the others can do and so lessons have to be taught in ways that do not benefit those with the technology.

Adam was in the quite unique position of having a few months of access to a class set of devices pretty much exclusively. He was able to keep them in his classroom, use them with a variety of classes, configure them in lots of different ways, trial different apps, different workflows, different teaching methods, all before sharing these findings with a small group of interested teachers for the next stage of the pilot. This access meant that Adam ironed out many of the kinks before anyone else knew about them; this is something he sees as pivotal and integral to the Director of Technology role and why a thorough and lengthy pilot reaps rewards in the long run. Before the initial pilot was over, he had already identified the shortcomings and requirements for the devices and could direct his attention accordingly. He hadn't resolved all of these issues by the time the school got to phase 2 of the pilot scheme, but was able to offer some reassurances and pre-empt certain questions because of this process.

However, it is important to note, that a 1-to-1 trial is not the same as having class sets; the devices are not built to be shared in this way and you are far less likely to get meaningful and transformational teaching with class sets because there is little momentum and consistency for teacher or student. If a 1-to-1 trial is not possible, then at least what is suggested above (one or two teachers using them as often as possible) will give you a closer picture of the reality of full mobile device integration.

This first phase allowed Adam to answer for himself many of the questions that would later be pivotal to winning support for the project and they largely came from the list of questions at the end of the Director of Technology section:

- Why are we making the move to mobile learning in THIS school?
- What is the right device for THIS school?
- What is the right timeframe for deployment for THIS school?
- What will good teaching and learning look like with a mobile device?
- Who from the staff are likely to champion this process?
- Who from the staff are likely to need the most encouragement or are likely to try to block this change?
- Is the infrastructure of the school ready to support this change?
- Is the technical support team right for this change?
- How can we involve the students in the process as early as possible?
- How will we measure the success of this project at various points in time?
- Beyond the device, what other changes will be introduced because of this initiative (i.e. cloud-based software, support for students with learning difficulties, the way exams are sat)?
- How will I engage with and get support from subject leaders?
- How will I engage with and get support from pastoral leaders?

Beyond these, a number of very specific questions will arise from this pilot to do with workflow and productivity.

Without a doubt, workflow is the part of the whole process of mobile technology integration that gets overlooked more than any other. In our opinion, workflow is everything; if you know how to get from A to B in the most efficient and potentially inspiring, potentially time-saving way, then you will not only win over staff who doubt the viability and usefulness of the technology, but you will also ensure that the students are confident in your ability to help guide them in this area. Please see Chapter 6 on Workflow for a detailed analysis of this area.

Once you've been through the early, investigative stages of piloting, it's time to move into working out if the project scales. For this reason, it's vital that Phase 2 of your pilot is designed to replicate as closely as possible the circumstances under which the full 1-to-1 will take place, albeit in a smaller scale, otherwise how is it going to help you? For example, too many of the pilots we've seen have borne little similarity to the project they precede. One teacher (usually the enthusiastic expert) gets an Apple TV and a class set of iPads and goes on to demonstrate what we already know - iPads can be really great in the hands of passionate, skilled educational technologists operating in the fairly placid waters of their own classroom.

Phase 2 of the pilot scheme in Adam's school was getting iPad Champions lined up (because, yes, after a lot of detailed trialling, it was concluded that this device was the most likely to deliver what the school needed). These were members of staff who were willing to have a mobile device and receive training in how to utilise it best in the classroom. This stage is another essential one in winning a whole staff body over to change.

If we use Roger's work on 'Technology Adoption' from his 'Diffusion of Innovations' paper in 1962 (see below) we may recognise more clearly the need and success of having a group of champions. If one considers the Headteacher, Network Manager and Director of Technology as the 'innovators' then the 'early adopters' are your iPad Champions.
If you're able to handpick your Champions, then the logical thing to do would be to pick all the super-keen teachers that jumped at the offer of a

'free iPad.' However, sometimes these are the people that lose interest the quickest, volunteer for everything or have forgotten that it was little Josie's birthday next week and might well have just solved the problem. The best possible combination for Champions is a range of subjects, age and teaching experience. It's very powerful to get people who have staffroom influence on board, and if you can get someone on Senior Management then all the better. It may surprise you to read that we would also recommend getting one or two of the naysayers involved as well. Often these are teachers that feel threatened by, or do not feel a part of the change and more often than not the decision they have reached about technology in the classroom is full of misconceptions. Giving these teachers the opportunity to test drive a new initiative gives you and them the freedom to honestly review and engage with change in a supportive, relatively low-pressure situation.

Having these 'champions' gives the opportunity for the Director of Technology to do two key things:

1. realise what questions he/ she had not answered/ had not realised needed asking
2. formalise and test any training that staff will be receiving later on in the rollout process.

Diffusion of Innovations[30]

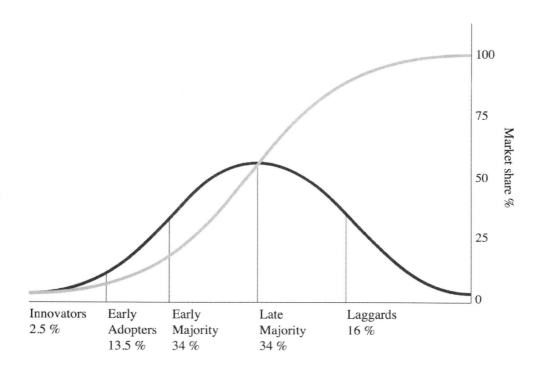

To a certain extent it may seem a given that one school may learn very effectively from another and the same must of course be true of pilot schemes. Indeed, as an institution that was leading the way in staff training in this field and with people asking the right questions, one could argue that many of the questions asked and answers found can simply be passed on as nuggets of wisdom for others to replicate.

In some respects this is true. One of the major hurdles encountered in early iPad pilots is a need to connect to a school's servers to access resources and documentation held centrally and often created originally on PCs. Early on, the only viable solution was to implement WebDAV, now there are a range of products on the market that can do this in a very user-friendly way.

[30] Rogers, E., 'Diffusion of Innovations', 5th Edition, Simon and Schuster, 2003.

Printing to networked printers from iPad was a headache, but again, companies are catching up with this, and it is as easy as if you were in your own home (please see the sections on Infrastructure and Joined-Up Systems for more detail).

But as one problem is solved, others will replace them and each school will have its own sticking points; things that key decision-makers will flag up as being essential to progress, Sometimes these will be well chosen, other times they may be pet-projects, but one way or another, we come back to having a strong Director of Technology and a clear vision; the proof of both, come from a well organised pilot scheme.

Applications are an important part of the pilot process. A successful pilot for example, will not be one centred around what we call 'one hit wonders;' apps that do one thing really well, but will actually only be useful to a subject teacher for one or two lessons a year. A successful pilot comes back to workflow, and on the iPad, workflow is about having a core set of applications that you can rely on to do the majority of the tasks you wish to do.

The pilot requires staff to road-test applications that do important jobs well. There are 7 key areas that are common to most teachers, so try to construct a range of workflow options for these:

1. Reading
2. Note-taking
3. Presentations
4. File-sharing
5. Research
6. Assessment
7. Marking & Feedback

If you can get your 'champions' to agree on the applications that best facilitate these requirements and, even better, can find a combination that complement one another effectively, then you will have achieved a great deal from your pilot.

So, as a minimum requirement, a pilot scheme should leave you clear about what your workflow is going to look like and what it is exactly that you envision the device being used for, so that you can pass this on to staff when you launch the project to them. This brings credibility to team leading the project and gives clear points of focus on how to move things forward. The reality is however, that technology never ceases in its development and that for the Director of Technology at least, the pilot never ends.

3.2.2   Staff launch

The pilot as described above, should probably last about a year. Perhaps, as previously alluded to, because many of the initial problems are being solved by others all the time, one could shrink this period a little, but we do not believe that a pilot scheme of less than 2 terms would be at all effective in preparing the 'early adopters' for the role they will need to play in assisting with the staff launch.

The pilot phase, combined with the almost certain need to up-scale your infrastructure, will restrict any school that wants this to succeed to a more leisurely timescale than some would like. Believe it or not, one of the many challenges that a Director of Technology will have to overcome is convincing the Head and other senior people to slow down. We are aware of many schools that have, or are rushing this, focused only on being 1-to-1 by September 201X. They'll reach that milestone, for sure, but it is less certain that their project will be sustainable educationally.

Indeed, once again, like a pilot, a staff launch is something many schools will overlook, and do so, at their peril.

One of the attributes you'll hear put forward about an iPad in particular, is that it is easy to use because of the intuitive nature of iOS and other tablet operating systems, for the most part. This is absolutely true; you can put the iPad into the hands of almost any child and within a short period of time they will have mastered it.

So does it then follow that you can put the iPad into the hands of teachers and expect the same results?

No.

If you give a child a device they will sit and play with it until you ask them to stop and perhaps even after that they'll still keep playing. If you give one to a teacher, they'll do what they can when they can, but it might well sit in a drawer for a long while before they get the opportunity to really test-drive it. Beyond the constraints of time, it is also worth remembering that there are plenty of teachers who learnt their trade in schools where technology simply didn't exist and many who don't see it's value.

This is for two reasons. Firstly, the overwhelming majority of teachers are success stories of the traditional system - they're perhaps the least psychologically well-equipped people to consider radical change in the education system, perversely enough. Secondly, technology is inherently risky. It might not work, and you've got GCSE results to worry about and the Head of Department breathing down your neck. Probably best not to rock the boat. Now where's that stack of worksheets and 2b pencils?

So, if the technology is valuable, and we believe it is, then it is the job of those that do have the knowledge to pass it on and ensure that they take as many other staff with them as possible.

If you're rolling out a 1-to-1 program, iPad or any other tablet for that matter, it is essential that what precedes this is a detailed, thoughtful training schedule for the staff. Without this, the project is likely to flounder or fail. A school's management cannot expect meaningful teaching and learning with technology to happen by simply handing out a device.

What often happens with a big deployment is that as part of the package schools will be offered a certain number of hours of training from external trainers. Apple, for example, give device suppliers approximately £400 per 50 iPads sold to provide a day's APD (Apple Professional Development). This, and schemes like it, can be a great way to kick start your campaign but it is not the conclusion. A few hours of support is simply not enough; the support needs come in-house on a day-to-day basis and not just from a technical perspective. Teachers need to know there is someone they can come to and say 'this is what I would like to do, is that possible?' And for the person they ask to be able to tell them yes or no, and 'this is how you could do it', to make sure staff are focusing on teaching and learning rather than just showcasing apps.

As has already been implied, too much training is about apps. Obviously apps are important, but building ideas for lessons around specific 'content' apps is a sure fire way to short-change your students. We think that teachers are better served being taught about a core set of tools that create a workflow that meets the majority of their needs. Beyond that there will be a need for personalised responses.

Technology has been hailed as giving the opportunity for individual, personalised learning. In order for that to happen teachers need to have received the same thing. If they can sit down with people they trust and talk through their options, discuss ideas they have, get help utilising the resources they already have and get support in their lessons and feedback after they've tried something new, then the use of technology will more likely be embedded into the culture of the school over time. This is where the 'champions' who have already done the training become essential agents of change. The Director of Technology and his/ her team, will of course lead the training, but one cannot overestimate just how powerful one 'novice' colleague giving hints and tips to another can be in making things happen in this arena. Opinion is still divided about what, if anything, Becta achieved in its short life, but one of its research findings that resonates is that the most effective technology CPD is delivered by credible peers in recognisable contexts.

In one of the authors' schools, every member of staff receives at least 7 hours of training in small groups over the course of about 3 months. They are getting this *before* the rollout of iPads so that they are prepared for what happens next. They have an environment where they are able to learn without the immediate pressure of putting it into practice before they've had the opportunity to evaluate what it is they want this new string to their bow to look like. They have access to a class sets of iPads that can be booked so they can experiment with what's being learnt, but the face-to-face training is also supported by an iTunes U course which goes over everything that is talked about in 'class'. This means that training can be scheduled *and* self-paced simultaneously. Teachers can pick out the things they like from one session and work this through to its conclusion and then come back to other things over the holidays when there is a bit of time to take on board other new ideas.

Beyond this, teachers also need to be able to drop in or be dropped in on to figure out what their next move is. This is where coaching and team teaching come in to play. It's hugely powerful and beneficial for staff to help each other as they go along this journey. Your 'champions' who have a bit more experience and confidence are your greatest resource in getting other staff on board. If they can go in to lessons with their peers and offer feedback that has absolutely nothing to do with 'judgement' and everything to do with offering a different point of view from someone who is just a few steps ahead on the learning curve, progress will be made more quickly, more smoothly and with a less intrusive feel about it.

In 2001, Marc Prensky introduced us to the concept of Digital Natives and Digital Immigrants.[31] Since then, the digital revolution has exploded and as such research has followed that suggests the theories behind the words may not hold up to scrutiny. However, the terms themselves provide a useful way of considering the student-teacher divide: teachers are 'natives' when it comes to teaching and learning; that is their language and they are fluent in it. It shouldn't come as a surprise that when learning a new language there is a need for intensive support, that there will be things that are lost in translation, some mispronunciations and frustrations. The flipside of this is that our students may feel like they are digitally superior in confidence and ability to their elders, but they still need to learn about how to harness this knowledge, and that is why they need our teachers to be trained up with this new and powerful technology before they are utilising it in schools.

Another crucial aspect of success takes us back to the Rogers diagram in the previous section. A project that is handled in the way being outlined,

---

[31] http://www.marcprensky.com/writing/Prensky%20-%20Digital%20Natives,%20Digital%20Immigrants%20-%20Part1.pdf

will not be derailed by the 'laggards' of his model. They may or may not 'convert' to using technology as an embedded part of their practice, but the point is that everyone else will and the opportunities have been given. Each school will have a different attitude to those that don't adopt technology when going down this mobile integration pathway, but what is important to remember is that for hundreds of years schools have accepted that individual teachers do things in their own individual ways. This will remain true even if every teacher in the world was given their own tablet technology. Some will adopt, some will not, but what will remain true is that the use of the device is limited only by the imagination of the teacher. Some will use it to turn fruit into musical instruments, some will use it to make instructional videos, some will use it to facilitate them sitting somewhere else in their classroom. Some won't use it at all. We think that all of these options are acceptable. Teaching and learning is not something homogenous. That's good. If introducing mobile technology in the school was going to change that, We would not wish to promote it.

Giving staff a 'lead-in' time to experiment with individual classes, or even lessons is a great way for them to become more confident and gives the Director of Technology further opportunity to explore different or changing options before reaching the student launches.

3.2.4   Student launches – incremental or Big Bang?

Getting everything in place for a 1-to-1 mobile device launch is a big task. Depending on your starting point it can takes months, maybe years of planning. Because of this, many schools get the finish line in sight and decide to pull the trigger as quickly as possible, handing out the devices they've spent so long preparing for, to all and sundry.

If the team leading this project are experienced, or the school has strong support from other schools or a network that oversees their progress, this might work, on a physical level. There are many things that can go wrong, lots of lessons to be learnt along the way. How problematic these are depends a little on how well you've prepared. Your bandwidth might not be up to speed; if you've given yourself room to grow then this won't ruin the project, but if you haven't, then you may be undone before you've even begun. The filtering will undoubtedly need a lot of tampering with - things that were blocked before are now unblocked and vice versa. Your MDM (Mobile Device Management) might start misbehaving when having to push out such large quantities of apps and the groupings you thought Active Directory would automatically create and copy over don't. All of these things can more can happen, but all are usually surmountable. Please see Mark's section on infrastructure for the detail on this vital area.

All In

The advantages of going 'all in' and putting a mobile device in the hands of each student is that you show faith and confidence in the infrastructure, the planning, the staff and your students all in one go. From a marketing point of view this is a great story and if all goes well then the school looks like a trailblazer and a school that knows how to navigate the next generation of technology and students in education. You also avoid the students who didn't get their device in the first wave being disgruntled, which in term should obviate the risk of internal theft. There is also a perceived advantage that teachers will be immediately forced into adapting to the technology, with nowhere to hide in this model of wholesale change.

The disadvantages stem from the same point - you're putting all your eggs in one basket and if there are problems, these will be across all students in all years. Even a small glitch can seem amplified by the fact that it happens in every class in every year group, even though it might only be for a few days. The traction a project like this gain often stems from the first few days and weeks of its existence in finished form. If your launch is not obviously successful you may lose potential support quite quickly. Neither staff or student is easily fooled and if they sense that you're pushing ahead with a project before it was fully conceived, then it will struggle to gain momentum. Teachers have a limited supply of faith to invest. Every small failure depletes this and if enough accrete as the product of a premature or too large a scale launch, they will suffer exhaustion and retrench to proven strategies. And who could argue with them for doing so?

A full launch is hard on staff. Again, the makeup of your school will heighten or lessen the truth of this statement, but if one takes an 'average' school in terms of its use of technology, what will be seen day-to-day is PCs being used by staff to do work or launch lesson content and Interactive Whiteboards being used with varying degrees of success at the front of classrooms. To move from this to a 1-to-1 environment is a big change.

Without doubt, one would expect pockets of outstanding and poor practice to sandwich the good practice that develops, but one runs the risk, with a quick wholesale change of this sort, of having more significant polarisation.

Incremental Change

The major advantage of incremental change is exactly what the name suggests; you get to ease into what is likely to be your school's most significant and expensive teaching and learning initiative in a very long time. As problems happen, they can be solved in a timely manner, safe in the knowledge that in the following years, when there are a higher volume of devices, you will not run into that same problem again, or at least you will have discovered a suitable workaround.

If you consider a typical secondary school with a sixth form, you will be dealing with students ranging from 11-18 years old. Within the time these students are at school, they change drastically as individuals. The way they are treated and taught also evolves as they progress through their school careers. A lesson with Year 7 is different (and rightly so) than a lesson with Year 13. So it is with technology and the way it is utilised in class. The primary benefits of a mobile learning device for Year 7 are different to how you will teach and they will learn with it as they get older. This puts additional strain on teachers who are trying to come to terms with the technology if you find every student on your timetable has a device. With an incremental change you can help teachers adjust to the different possibilities over a more significant period of time.

We would propose for example, that a school that started with Year 7 and Year 12 in their first year of rollout, would reap all the rewards of seeing the different capabilities of a mobile learning device without the added complication of suddenly having all the exam years with devices, understanding what is possible or appropriate with each different year group and trying to establish whether they would use the core apps that they are familiar with in different ways with each class they teach.

Instead, a Year 7 and 12 start means that the majority of teachers are catered for (those who specialise in Key Stage 3 and A Level teaching are both accommodated) and there is still plenty of breathing space for those that are not yet feeling confident. Similarly, immediately introducing devices to Years 10-11 is very high risk. Schools are likely to have evolved delicate formulae for maximising students' exam success. Introducing a 1-to-1 rollout into that formula may indeed produce change; the kind of change a hand-grenade brings...

In a way this first year is an extension of the trial; it gives plenty of scope for mistakes to be made, for policies to be honed and infrastructure to be improved. Whilst the aim is to have to do none of this, the reality is that it is unlikely to be perfect straightaway, and frankly it is a useful mindset to adopt to consider any and every part of your project as something that will evolve constantly. The devices will get better and change, your usage and needs with regards to Wi-Fi will increase and the goals for your project will adapt over time. There is no need to rush this process as in many ways you are not driving towards a finish line, so much as helping the on-going process of evolution that all schools should be striving for.

The disadvantages of incremental change are mostly to do with timing. If you are under pressure to complete the project then this is obviously not the right approach for you. There is no shame and indeed, as we have explained above, there are huge advantages to taking it slowly with such a large project, but the reality is that schools are under pressure to make changes and in an increasingly competitive marketplace, this is more and more the case. Other possible disadvantages revolve around giving opportunities to second guess and undermine the project by not fully committing to it. If you label this year as a trial you leave yourself open to criticism and derailment in a way that a quick wholesale change would not. Nonetheless, constructive feedback during a project's formative years is often beneficial and aids the long-term development of the work being done.

Section 3.3 The importance of the right device

3.3.1   Which device?

Choosing the right device is a critical part of the process of engaging with mobile technology in the classroom. There are so many options of device and so many different ways your project could take shape. In this section we are thinking about physical considerations, but often these link in to other more philosophical questions about what you're trying to achieve in a more holistic sense. It is worth noting that although device choice shouldn't be an Achilles heel, it really is. Almost all 1-to-1 projects prior to the release of the iPad failed, because the devices available were:

- too heavy;
- lacking decent battery life;
- very boring and focused purely on 'work';
- poorly functional.

The advent of modern tablet computers has solved all of these issues. What makes things more complicated is that when you compare statistics then largely they all look quite similar. Pretty much every mainstream tablet has a screen size of between 7 & 12 inches, they all weigh less than a kilogram and many not even half that. There are really only 3 operating systems to consider as well; iOS, Android and Windows. To throw in another option, you can still look at the option of laptops. Here though you're still limited to three options: Windows, Apple and Chromebook. So how different can they all be?

Well the answer is that partly it depends what you want them to do and what your expectations are. The cost, the build quality and the usability can vary far more and with the exception of cost, these are things you only discover when the device is in your hand and you're trying to make it work for you.

Android tablets are the most variable because so many different companies have the opportunity to utilise the Android OS. Samsung has been a fairly clear winner in the market with regards to education and the Galaxy Tab series has pushed the iPad just about as hard as anyone, but not in the educational arena. Microsoft have stumbled repeatedly to launch a tablet and indeed operating system that people wish to buy into and, whilst the Surface Pro is a good device, it is not finding its way into schools because the pedigree in the tablet market simply isn't there. There's no doubt that when it comes to desktop computers, Microsoft have been the outright leader for as long as anyone can remember, but in terms of innovation in this field, the offerings have missed the mark, certainly with schools. Their most appealing option functionally cost in excess of £1000 a unit, which puts it on a par with a MacBook Pro in terms of cost, but not in terms of power or ergonomics. The other options simply don't work in a way that a user finds appealing, indeed in a way that users find, well, usable.

It seems that just as one schools have always invested in Windows PCs, the same is now true of the Apple iPad. Whilst to a certain extent statistics released by companies need to be treated with a pinch of salt, it is hard to ignore that in the USA, Apple have a 94% market share of the tablet market in schools and in the UK, the trend seems to be similar. A recent report by BESA[32] suggests that the facts are slightly different to the marketeering headlines. However, what we can see is that in the UK, 75% of schools have an eye on going 1-to-1 and given it is projected that by the end of 2015, the iPad will account for around 34% of the devices in schools. It is hard to gauge how this compares to the projected 42% market share for 'Google Android' as this accounts for such a wide variety of devices, but it certainly seems that the iPad is, and will continue to be at the top of many lists for which device to choose.

Why is this? Apple have created a product that is absolutely usable, of a high build quality and the App Store is significantly more appealing to schools, both for the range of apps it offers, but also its security (something that the Android stores really struggle with - although their Play for Education store may change this). It also comes in two sizes (with a larger

---

[32] http://www.besa.org.uk/sites/default/files/tab2013_0.pdf

12.9 inch screen rumoured to launch in Spring 2015) that suit two different markets, whilst giving a consistently high quality experience.

Apple has invested significantly in education and the support of iTunes U and software packages like iBooks Author offer significant rewards and benefits to teachers and schools that are willing to invest in this ecosystem (of which more later).

Many schools that have considered the Android operating system have found that there are some fundamental problems that Apple devices don't suffer from. Most critically, the ungate-kept app store, allowing access to all manner of inappropriate, risky, illegal and poor-quality content. Similarly, because of the enormous variety of devices which use Android (unlike Apple, Google allow anyone to make the hardware), apps can be unstable or function poorly as it's impossible to optimise them for every screen size and hardware configuration. Both of these problems are in the process of being fixed as there's now a Google Play for Education store which handles quality control, but it's only available on a tiny number of devices, such as Samsung's Tab 4 Education. Android is perceived as being cheap, but once devices are specified to match an iPad, from a premium manufacturer, with a decent screen and capable of accessing Play for Education, the saving is minor. The fact that Android is the operating system of choice for many smartphone users may hint towards an easier adoption curve, once the educational proposition is as mature as Apple's.

With reference to laptops, although I outlined three options, Apple do not offer an affordable option for most schools, which really rules them out of contention (and frankly, the iPad offers more versatility for a student than the MacBook range). A Windows laptop is unlikely to ruffle too many feathers in the IT office, however, it is also unlikely to set many student hearts on fire. Whilst this may seem like a superficial point, student buy-in is probably the single most important factor in the success of a 1-to-1 implementation. If the students don't respect the device, they will not use them in the way you want them to and may not use them at all. Similarly, a Windows laptop is not designed with innovation in mind; it does what a desktop does and little to nothing extra, aside from the portability aspect.

Maintaining the status quo rather defeats so many of the possible gains of a mobile device rollout and as such, this seems like a poor choice.

The Chromebook however, is a rather more interesting option, as it gets as close as we currently can to the idea of BYOB (Bring Your Own Browser). The hardware itself is less important than what Google is offering through GAFE (Google Apps for Education), of which you can find out more in Section 6.2

Irrespective of device, certain things remain true and necessary when considering your device. In secondary school you need a screen size of at least 9 inches to have enough space to see and do all that one would expect to achieve. You simply can't be expected to label a complex diagram or write an essay on a screen any smaller than this. There would also be a significant disadvantage to those students who have larger hands when using a smaller virtual keyboard. However, a smaller screen and weight (and lower cost) may well suit a primary setting. What is also important is ensuring that the device is well protected in a substantial case. Certainly in a primary setting the case should be drop proof. A good case does not negate the need for a high build quality; Apple, Samsung and Microsoft all know how to make a device that is robust and substantial in the hand, even if it weighs next to nothing.

Primary schools actually have some tricky decisions when it comes to device selection. A smaller, lighter device seems to be the obvious choice, especially as this will invariably mean it will be cheaper and primary budgets are usually more stretched than anybody else's. However, there is a counter-argument which suggests that young students, who have less refined motor skills may well benefit from more screen space. At this point there needs to be a serious plan of action for primary schools leaders; this is a big investment and apps aimed at primary schools are limited in their longevity. They are good for a few minutes in a lesson, but unlike secondary schools which will utilise word processing apps and presentation tools regularly throughout the day, primary schools need to ensure that they are going to get a good return on their investment. If a smaller, cheaper device has a good camera, a robust case, the range of applications that work well, then think carefully about spending more than necessary.

Whilst it is important that a tablet device is light in the hand and the bag, the reality is that they will be on desks as much as they will be in hands, so it is not the only or indeed primary consideration. That said, the Microsoft Surface Pro is by far the heaviest device and because of its desire to be a laptop and tablet it is larger and heavier than all of the other devices available by some margin and would not be very useful in lessons where 'mobile' was the operative word, and certainly younger students would really struggle to make this device work for them. Frankly, if you want what Windows 8 offers - the familiarity of Windows and Office - then there are better devices, indeed better types of device. In this scenario we would opt for a lightweight laptop rather than compromise with the tablet-version of Windows 8. But a larger and more philosophical point bears some thought - you've been using Windows and Office in your school for years. Are you after more of the same, or are you trying to achieve something different? What at first appears a strength (familiarity) may actually be a weakness (inertia).

Every interface has its own quirks and nuances and yet they are also beginning to align. As one company releases a particularly popular tweak, so it will follow (with a different name) on rival devices as soon as possible. That said, it can still all go horribly wrong, as seen with Windows 8 and the failure to win over customers to this 'tablet-friendly' interface. And, whilst education specific apps (of which one should constantly be a little suspicious and skeptical about anyway) are beginning to appear on Windows 8, they lag behind iOS and Android significantly (tens of thousands against over half a million).

Yet again iOS wins the battle for its simplicity, free updates and upgrades and its accessibility functions both for those with disabilities and those who are simply not that tech-savvy. Latest iOS 8 accessibility functions include:

- Voiceover - describes everything that is happening on the screen
- Speak Screen - will read text back to you, such as email or web pages
- Zoom - a built in magnifier that works for anything on screen
- Dictation mode
- Invert colours and grayscale

- Dynamic font adjustment

These features set iOS apart as they build on the already outstanding functions that Apple have incorporated since iOS 5.

iOS is recognisable by students and staff alike and those that don't know it find it a simple transition, (far more so than the move from Windows to OSX for example). The biggest challenge with iOS is that it does not utilise the folder system that those born and bred on Windows will recognise and feel comfortable with. In some respects this is where a system like Google Apps for Education comes in as a factor. Google Apps is entirely free for education and offers cloud-based word processing, presentation and spreadsheet tools as well as the most honed and usable 'collaboration' features of any platform out there. The fact that it can be used on any platform (iOS, Android or Windows) is a big bonus for those that may consider a mixed economy (more of this later).

There are a range of options for schools when choosing a device. Sometimes cost will be a deciding factor, other times it will be personal preferences of those in decision-making positions. But when all is weighed and measured there are actually very few truly capable devices. And when you look at the choice between going with an option that is pervasive and well-supported, gaining traction and supporters all the time and then at the option of utilising something that may initially seem more familiar, or less expensive or different, it seems counter-intuitive to choose the lesser, more obscure option without having strong pedagogical reasons to motivate such a decision. The fact that most schools have thus far opted for the iPad is often derided as bandwagon jumping. However, We've yet to come across a school that has made this decision for any reason other than an educational one, following extensive investigation of the alternatives. Sometimes market trends indicate the wisdom of the crowd, and we think that's true in this case.

Choosing the right device: a checklist of questions, actions and choices

- Will you be using the device in a 1-to-1 environment?
- Are you willing to move away from a Microsoft desktop environment?
- Are you trying to make access of PowerPoint more mobile, or are you after something different?
- Is screen size more important than touchscreen capability?
- How important is portability - will students need to carry the device everywhere?
- Is your network ready to take Bonjour traffic, or indeed any non-windows traffic?
- Will all students of all ages use the same device?
- Do different Key Stages require access to different tools or interfaces?
- Have you taken a test-drive with a range of devices?
- Have you let students loose on the devices you're considering?
- Have you got student feedback and input on what they want?
- Have you visited schools that are already going 1-to-1?
- Have you looked at the workflows in place when using different devices?
- Do you know if you could support the workflows you find appealing?

3.3.2   Ecosystem

The term 'ecosystem' refers to the software environment, apps and tools that the surround the device. The ecosystems on offer, as with the devices that represent them, are similar in many ways. When buying a device for individual use, part of the process comes down to personal preferences, but with a device that will be used in schools, the way the choice is made and why is more complex.

Most schools continue to operate in a Microsoft Windows ecosystem. For reasons of finance and familiarity, it seems unlikely that this will change anytime soon. Despite the idealism that some mobile learning supporters will preach, schools do still need desktop computers and will probably continue to do so for some time yet. If nothing else, much of the administration done in schools is dependent on desktop computers that are networked in a specific way and to try to remove this would probably be counterproductive. Similarly, there are still things that tablet computers cannot do and complex software that requires more processing power does, for the moment, need to be stored and run on a more powerful machine. At secondary level, specialist subject use in music, DT, art and computer science are immediately obvious areas where this is the case. Some primaries, however, have gone completely 'ICT-room free'.

So, if you're running in a Microsoft ecosystem, the obvious choice would be to continue with that? Yes and no. Yes it would be easy for your technical support team to make this happen. In all likelihood this is the option that they would favour because it keeps a system that is well known to them. However, if you buy into the Microsoft ecosystem at tablet level then you are also buying into Windows 8 which many schools are not upgrading to, partly because lots of legacy application will not run on it. Also, Windows 8 is a significantly different user experience than the previous versions so there is still a period of adjustment for staff and other users which largely negates the argument that the user experience will be uninterrupted and the same as it has always been. Similarly, with the introduction of Microsoft Office 365, the continued use of Microsoft Office is available on any platform, not just a Windows one, which again trumps any arguments based on familiarity, because this can be transferred with you.

This means that the things teachers are familiar and happy with, such as Microsoft Word, can be used on any machine, anywhere, anytime and this continuity is one of the most important aspects of mobile learning; if you can't jump from one device to another and pick up where you left off, then we would suggest that the ecosystem isn't working properly. Please see the section on Joined-Up Systems below for more detail.

Google and Apple both have solutions that work well in supporting the battle for continuity and make powerful cases for being your primary ecosystem. Google Apps for Education (GAFE) is a particularly powerful setup as the whole thing is free from start to finish and utilises a system that many are familiar with. From Docs to Calendar, everything lives in the same system and the way GAFE is set up means that your students are automatically connected to you, unlike systems such as Edmodo and Showbie which require students to sign up using course codes. GAFE is a highly user-friendly system that has been developed from the commercial elements that are enjoyed by millions of users worldwide. What is highly appealing about this system beyond the price tag, is that it is genuinely cross-platforms and highly customisable for schools. An institution can have its own domain, emails and with the introduction of Google Classroom, many of the traditional requirements of a VLE are replaced and exceeded. One cautionary note with GAFE, is that whilst the user experience improves constantly, it is a system designed with Chromebooks in mind and is a slightly more laptop-friendly than it is for a tablet. We take an extended look at these options in the chapter on Workflow.

Apple's iCloud system means that it is now possible to use the iWorks apps (Pages, Numbers and Keynote) on a PC through a web browser. By logging in to iCloud.com you will have access to all documents created on your Apple devices (as long as you have turned iCloud on). This system offers the lowest amount of free storage of the three main options, but offers the advantage of native apps that are genuinely built for tablet use, combined with a web editor that has all the functionality you would expect on a PC. If you use an iCloud email address and the calendar, then these too are synced with this login. You can also use your iCloud account to find your device if it is lost using 'find my iPad' as well as remotely wipe the device if you believe it is lost. By doing this, you would still have access to all of your documents, as they are stored in iCloud. The usability of the apps on iPad is what sets the iCloud system apart from its competitors, but it does not have the universality of GAFE in the range of applications available using this service and certainly doesn't have as much free storage as Office 365.

None of these options are perfect and none of them offer you a completely fool proof solution that does not require some sort of alternative or backup. You cannot achieve everything you want using GAFE alone; this system needs to be supported by other applications and the availability of these will depend upon the devices you choose to run GAFE on. Office 365 seems to be very good at what it does, but as part of a Windows package is short on innovation. iCloud only allows you access to limited number of applications remotely, however it does backup all of the content on your device, so if it were lost, you could be up and running with an exact replacement within an hour or so.

If we look at the possibilities of Android and Apple more generally we see two systems that are becoming more alike - Apple is slowly opening itself up to more developers and allowing small margins of freedom that were not there before and Android is beginning to get the top-class content that has been on the Apple platform for some time. The risk with Android remains the openness of its system. It allows content that would never make it through the strict censorship that Apple runs, which means that there is some very poor and potentially dangerous content in its stores. Conversely, Apple frustrates developers and users by not allowing as much freedom and customisation, whether this is in imposing security settings or making a more personalised interface. However, over the short course of mobile learning history, Apple's ecosystem has without doubt dominated and much of the reason for this is the quality content that is available and the seamless way in which it is delivered.

Some have criticised Apple's proprietary nature, raising the spectre of schools investing heavily (in terms of their intellectual capital) by making resources in iTunes U or ePub format that will be hard to use in other systems, should they want to jump ship in future. This is a fair criticism, and its a measured risk that schools have to judge. Is the richness and functionality of the format worth the trade off? As you can export all that stuff to PDF (not exactly interactive, but universally viewable), the risk severity is slightly lower than some people would have you believe.

The gold-standard in ecosystem terms is one which is truly device agnostic - one which lets your staff and pupils view and exchange content and apps without having to own a specific piece of hardware. This will become increasingly important as schools begin to experiment with multi-device strategies (e.g. iPad at KS2-3, Chromebook at KS4-5 - see the section immediately below).

Over time the differences between the various ecosystems will likely diminish, but at present Apple has the pedigree and investment in education that puts it as the lead in terms of platform, but certainly Google are making a very powerful and important statement with their software which is used in an overwhelming majority of American institutions.

The answer to the question of where to place one's allegiance is increasingly complex in so much as there are a wealth of options, but also because there is probably not one right answer. But don't worry, it's not as binary a decision as once it was, and many 1-to-1 schools use iOS as their base, supplementing its functionality with GAFE or O365.

3.3.3   A mixed economy?

What one learns from the previous section is that there are a number of great options for schools and users. The most important consideration at this stage is to ask oneself, at what point do I want to limit my options and make specific and unchanging choices?

Is one device for all students right? Is one platform for all users the right option? Should everyone be using the same word processing software?

It would be easy if the answer to all of those questions was 'yes' and for us to simply list the answers for you. However, the worlds of technology and education do not work like that. One way of learning doesn't suit every child, one device doesn't work perfectly in every situation. The trick here is to select the option which best fits your circumstances with the information you need to make that decision.

Very few schools are in a position where they could completely and utterly buy in to one ecosystem to the exclusion of all others, unless it were one based on Microsoft Windows. Financially and logistically, a change of this scale would be hugely challenging while the cost of the necessary infrastructure for mobile learning is still weighing heavy. This does not mean that some institutions won't strive to achieve this, at least over time, but it does mean that realistically, one ecosystem is unobtainable and frankly undesirable for many schools.

What is often seen, even within institutions that have a healthy budget, is that administrations staff and teaching staff operate on two different systems. This can work and because documentation between the two doesn't overlap very often, this is a realistic goal. The students in this scenario will have the same device or be using the same ecosystem as the teachers - that's a necessity.

However, what about the option of not having a common ecosystem at all? Bring Your Own Device (BYOD) brings huge benefits to schools where budgets are tight but where there is a desire to harness the power of mobile learning. However, with this approach come several significant barriers to genuine success. The primary problem with BYOD is that it is not one based on parity. Everything about the school system (rightly or wrongly) is based around children being given an equal opportunity, at least within their own setting. Students wearing a uniform is one example of this - no child can stand out (easily) as being more or less wealthy than another when the outfit is the same and so it goes with technology which can be a great leveller, or in the case of BYOD an incredibly divisive thing. If one student can have access to the latest device but another is only able to afford an almost obsolete model, then the school has not helped either of those students and the teaching and learning outcomes will be greatly reduced.

Similarly, whilst more and more applications and pieces of software are becoming cross-platform, in a BYOD classroom, the utilisation of said apps can be hindered because not everyone has access to the same technology. Whilst some may argue that this is mirroring a real-life situation where a student may be forced to problem-solve, you could also say that you are stretching a teacher's resourcefulness and ability to facilitate learning for all if there must constantly be a backup plan or a workflow that is a compromise because of the limits set by a BYOD classroom. Indeed these limits could shift from class to class and week to week as students change technology. This sort of a demand is difficult for a teacher to keep up with and realistically, only an already engaged and tech-savvy teacher is going to be motivated enough to face such a challenge. BYOD definitely has its place in education; in higher education it seems entirely relevant as students are taking far more control over their own learning and shared learning experiences seem to be largely web-based. In the secondary and primary classroom a BYOD policy can be fantastic for getting web access to all (and therefore utilising a plethora of web-based applications), but it can be hindered by complications and limited to being what one might call and one trick pony.

So the secondary and primary classroom would probably benefit from an approach which offers more consistency in terms of the devices used. This does not mean that a 'one for all' approach is the only solution however. You could decide that one device was more suitable for one stage of a child's education and a different one for another. For example, there is some merit in the idea of tablets for students up to the point where they need to prepare for public examinations and then a laptop or Chromebook for older students. In a way this panders to the exam system rather than reacts to what would be better for their overall education, but perhaps at present that is a moot point; exams are sat, and prepared for, in a specific way and it is going to take some time to change this.

One could opt for a model where a specific range of devices is acceptable, meaning that the school and its teachers are aware of what commonality there is between devices and can prepare and plan accordingly. This will work particularly well if there are cross-platform tools embedded into the process like Office 365, GAFE, Edmodo etc.

There is no doubt that technically speaking a BYOD policy can be very simple for a network manager to run if it is kept very separate from everything else and only Internet access needs to be provided; a Windows-based environment would probably be preferable and then at the bottom of the pile would be a single device that is not Windows-based. However, it is important to realise when making these decisions that 'difficult' is by no means 'impossible' and the spreading of the necessary knowledge is getting better, more accurate and is more readily available. A few years ago there was virtually no one in education who could get 100 iPads to play nicely on a Windows network, now this is happening all over the country. The technical side of things must not be the driving force when deciding what one's 1-to-1 project looks like. Equally, an old fashioned desire for uniformity or a laissez-faire approach needs to be considered carefully.

There is no right answer in amongst all of this debate, purely because every school has a different personality and goal. Some schools will be implementing change to drive results up, some will be using it as a way to prepare students for later life, some have teachers who are tech-savvy, others won't, most have some of both. What is important is that the project is not designed around a device or technical paper tigers.

Devices change. They upgrade, they get better (and worse) and competition increases all the time. What is the right decision now, may not be the right decision in two or three years' time. If your project is built upon the right principles, then it will continue to flourish even if you change device. And the key to that is making a sensible, informed decision over ecosystem. If a mixed approach to devices is likely (and we can't see many schools not wanting this option, in the medium-term), then an ecosystem that allows content and workflow to function agnostic of hardware choice is essential.

In order to make sure this happens, build your project around people and education, not technology and hardware. If you choose cloud storage that is not tied to a device, a platform that can be logged into anywhere anytime and you train teachers to use technology in its broadest sense, then you will create a school where the transition from one device to another will be fluid and straightforward and where tools remain tools - a means to achieving useful and meaningful things, rather than a system that acts to harness and restrict students and teachers from reaching their true potential.

4 FINANCE

Section 4.1 You want *how much?!?*

An effective 1-to-1 scheme, with the concomitant investment in staff development and infrastructure (see later in this chapter), will cost the 'average' secondary school of 1000 pupils approximately £500,000 over two to three years. Just take a brief pause to let that number sink in.

The figure of £500,000 is often met with snorts of derision by people (the more technical, the more derisive the snort, usually) who are convinced they can do it for less. In fact, the phrase often heard next is 'Actually our wireless is pretty good.' (For final clarity, it isn't good enough – see Section 5.2). However, when you tot up the various things that schools budget for during the lifetime of the project (audio visual streamers, secure storage, applications, insurance… the list stretches on and on), and the things that they don't (cabling, increased broadband, wireless refresh, CPD… this list goes on too), the final amount is rarely far off £500k.

The first important message that this enormous number should convey is that a 1-to-1 project should not be embarked on casually. It should not be devolved to that Assistant Principal who likes gadgets. It isn't something any school should 'experiment' with. This scale of investment dwarfs anything you've ever done with technology in the past and is probably only surpassed in magnitude by capital-financed building projects the school may occasionally have benefited from. That means that it has to succeed.

It is helpful to look at things from the viewpoint of someone who is not convinced that technology deployed in this way can be impactful. Consider what else you could achieve by spending half a million pounds over two to three years; the school could employ several extra teachers; class sizes could be reduced; you could finally buy that electron-scanning microscope the science department has been writing unconvincing business cases about for the last decade. There's no firm evidence for any of that stuff making any difference, by the way, but that's the case for technology too (see the section on research above).

Ignoring the hyperbolic tone of that last paragraph, the point is still worth noting – lots of people are going to be angry, oppositional or, at the very least, professionally skeptical about what you're proposing. So you better be secure in your decision, clear on what the evidence says and committed to the pedagogical and curricular changes it will bring. We refer you back to the opening chapter on visioning and the sections on leadership – deep, distributed and detailed decision-making is required. A project worth half a million pounds feels too big to fail in reputational, learning and (if it's public money) moral terms – but fail they do, repeatedly, and usually because of a failure to fully culture the organization around them.

Lecture over. You came here to find out about how to finance your project, not get hectored by some superannuated mortgage advisor.

Section 4.2 Where to find the money

There are several approaches to funding a 1-to-1 project, and we list them in ascending order of likelihood;

4.2.1 Increase fees; the ultimate contribution scheme

Independent schools are quite lucky in this respect, with a fee-collection mechanism already in place and a culture where parents are broadly accepting of the need to opaquely fund everything the school does. Independent schools we've worked with have found that a combination of an upfront investment in infrastructure followed by a modest (1%) fee increase ensures the financial viability of their scheme ad infinitum. Obviously this is harder than it sounds as independents operate in a fiercely competitive and (generally) shrinking marketplace, so it will need careful commercial consideration. Independent schools are sometimes tempted to separate provision of a device from the general school fee (but we've never got to the bottom of why) – this gives parents the chance to opt out, reduces the chance the change will succeed and brings in an otherwise absent administrative burden and should therefore be avoided.

4.2.2 Reserves; the war chest approach

Most state-funded schools operate within their budget year-on-year and slowly build a reserve from their revenue. Academies, particularly those who academised early when it seemed that the DfE was run by your indulgent uncle with the big cheque book, may have quite substantial sums salted away – we've seen reserves that run into the low millions. An operating reserve is obviously prudent, the massive, systemic under spending of money granted for specific pupils' education is something quite different, but we'll leave the ethical tightrope walking to you. If your school is in this position, fantastic; 1-to-1 is that rainy day you've been saving for. Plan early, build a war chest to take the sting out of the biggest bills, but bear in mind that sustainability past the initial wave will require something in addition (see below).

4.2.3 Sweating your assets & changing practices

This is linked to the building of reserves. When you consider that a successful 1-to-1 will obviate the need for 90% of your current IT estate (PCs, printers, laptops, servers) it makes sense to stop replacing this stuff, put the money somewhere ring-fenced and hobble on for as long as you can with your current assets. It's the equivalent of living with your parents for a couple of extra years while you save for a deposit for your own house; unpleasant and likely to lead to arguments about the remote, but ultimately forgotten once you're in your own place.

4.2.3.1   PCs/ Macs

These will only be needed for specific tasks, typically in technical subjects such as music, art and computer science as almost everything a pupil does day-to-day with technology at the moment will be done using their own device in the future. If your school is like most others, you will currently operate and cyclically replace multiple rooms full of the things. You know, the rooms where people go 'to do computers'. The nature of these rooms (hermetically sealed from wider cultures of learning, available only when the timetable not the need dictates, invariably fraught with minor technical hurdles) doesn't support effective use of technology for learning anyway, just an endless conveyor belt of PowerPoint presentations where the animation has had greater scrutiny than the content. Perhaps it's time to slowly remove the oldest one each term and create an appetite for rich, impactful tech which the current diet of beige boxes suppresses but doesn't satisfy?

4.2.3.2   Bookable laptops

Always a recipe for inflated expectations of mobile learning followed by the slough of despond (10 minutes to log on to the network, guessing which levered-off keys hide your password characters only for the battery to run out just as you get the wireless to wake up? No thanks), they will serve no purpose in your new environment. IT support will ultimately thank you too – laptop repairs are a significant overhead for them, probably 50%+ of their workload if you have multiple class-sets. Laptops are the classic example of a poorly suited technology being shoehorned into schools. Just think about the care with which you steward your own laptop's battery, screen and case to keep it working well. Now remove that sense of ownership and shove 300 of them into the melee of school life… Say it out loud now: I commit to never buying another Windows laptop for shared use.

4.2.3.3 Printers

A school at which one of the authors was an AP had over 200 printers of various vintage and manufacturer. Most had been purchased using departmental budgets from supermarkets – at least that's what their quality, specification and running costs would suggest. The school also used 1,000,000 sheets of A4 paper per year, which is a frightening measure of institutional dependence on the worksheet. When a school moves fully 1-to-1, in a thought-out and culturally embedded manner, with a good workflow and on-screen marking, the need to make a hard copy of work will decline exponentially. Work will be created, submitted, shared, commented on, marked, celebrated and then archived digitally.

It's quite tricky to make a saving here because people are so dependent on and wedded to the idea of holding a hard copy of documents. Admit it, you're reading this in printed form aren't you? It will require genuine strength of leadership, but it's really, *really* important; beyond the saving achieved through not replacing printers, ink or paper, there is also the need to prepare people culturally for not relying on paper. A big part of a successful 1-to-1 is having all staff planning for full use of the devices. If it remains possible to opt out and revert to 'worksheets and textbooks', many will, and this will weaken your efforts to embed change.

People will tell you that they *need* to print. They will beg you to see the uniqueness of their role and why the £50 Lexmark inkjet on their desk is integral to any and every school improvement effort. They must be resisted, with respect and empathy of course, but resisted nonetheless. Empathy isn't one of our greatest strengths – the AP in question went round the building when everyone had gone home and put all the printers in the skip.

What is required is nothing short of a whole-school edict – all printing must go through some kind of metered, rationed system (pull-printing to two or three strategically positioned devices is best) and no-one should be allowed to buy printers, paper or ink using discretionary funds they have access to. There are other potential sources of savings currently tied up in soon-to-be-obsolete paper products (pupil homework diaries being a common one), but we will merely mention this and move on, as this is peculiar to each school. Section 5.5 in below covers the issue of printing from tablets.

4.2.3.4   Servers

If you're doing it right (see the section on Joined-Up Systems below), the software and, most critically, everyone's files will no longer be provisioned in what technical folk like to call an on-premises TIA-compliant secure environment. The rest of us know it as the server cupboard. Free-to-education services from Google and Microsoft now make it a no-brainer to move your storage into the secure cloud and to stop buying, upgrading, housing, servicing, air-conditioning, supporting and generally pouring money into school-owned server rooms. Not only is this a huge saving, it actually works better too, with students able to access and share files from any device, anywhere, yet still with the security offered by a school-managed identity.

That all sounds great on the page, but it is actually quite hard to find real money from this approach. The only way to realize these theorized savings is to carry out a full analysis of your current costs, taking into account the softer costs around contracts and staffing. This analysis – and the proposed saving measures – should be presented to SLT and agreed, and part of this agreement needs to be that the sums identified as savings in each year are put aside and ring-fenced for the 1-to-1 project.

This is important because without buy-in throughout the senior team, changes to practice around printing and potentially also servers will be easily undermined. You will also need to evaluate the success of the savings measures, perhaps having agreed at sign-off a sliding scale of claw back based on how successfully you implement your changes.

4.2.4   Pupil Premium and other allowances

Maintained schools that have eligible pupils (and we'd guess that's every maintained school) receive funding associated with specific pupils who meet certain measures of need/ deprivation. Pupil Premium is the most widespread, as the bar is fairly low for this, but children with special needs, disabilities and who are Looked After will also attract additional funding. The way in which these monies are spent and the impact on the individual child will often need to be justified and in terms of access, digital divide and enhanced life chances, it doesn't get much more impactful than 1-to-1.

Notwithstanding the fact that this funding will already have been spent eleventy-seven times this year, it's worth bidding for a proportion this income in future budget rounds. When designing contribution schemes (see below), it is vital to make them affordable to every family and for this reason alone there is a strong argument for using Pupil Premium money to reduce the cost to those children who qualify.

It is also worth noting that Children Looked After (it generates a less judgmental acronym than Looked After Children, we are told) often have specific funding tied up at the Local Authority. In a previous scheme one of the authors ran, the LA were very keen that all CLA benefited and hence they paid for their devices outright.

As a yardstick, it may help to understand that most maintained 1-to-1 schools put in about 30% of their 'own' money (e.g. capital and/ or revenue) and seek to recover the remaining 70% from parental contributions.

4.2.5   Contributory schemes

We have yet to come across the 1-to-1 in a maintained school that did not ask for parental contributions in one form or another and this is for the simple reason that it brings a lot of benefits, as well as some minor headaches.

The idea isn't a complex one (parents make a monthly contribution to the scheme and in return their child gets a device) but the nuances are many and will require careful consideration before applying to your context. Firstly, let's deal with the upside;

- Even with no school investment in the cost of pupil devices (and the cases, insurance, apps et cetera that are required), a tablet-based scheme can usually be delivered over 3 years for somewhere around £10-15 per pupil per month, with a final optional payment to keep the device. Forgive the generalization, but this is quite attractive to parents as, effectively, is like buying a tablet on credit but: for less than they'd pay in the shops; minus the VAT (if your school can reclaim VAT); without attracting interest and; with the added benefit that their child's education will be enhanced.

- The act of making a contribution, regardless of the legal niceties which we'll go into later, confers ownership in the mind of the contributor. They feel the device is theirs and this is useful for many reasons. Firstly, the device will be looked after much better than if it had just been given for nothing. We need the children to care for these devices, to manage them, to charge them, to keep them safe from damage and, vitally, not to sell them on eBay. Secondly it creates a sense of investment and partnership in the project educationally, particularly if you repeatedly strike the right tone in your letters and presentations to parents. Having the pupils and their parents supporting this change is a massive boost. Finally, and this may not be that important in your context, 'ownership' puts a modern computer at the disposal of the family, not just the child. 1-to-1 schools report improved home-school communications and demand from parents for training.

- It makes your scheme affordable and sustainable, year after year. If the case is made to parents that the school is investing significant educational capital in change, and financial capital in infrastructure, it is credible that they should help with the addition of a screen and a processor. This amounts to assisted, common-platform BYOD, with the all of the problems associated with the 'Y' removed. Our current model of 1-to-1 provision is transitional – to make it effective, we have to dictate device type and impose software management – but within five years we believe the sector will have transitioned to a BYOB (the final B is for Browser) model, where the school provides infrastructure and licenses the software, which is all delivered through the browser to any cheap screen that a child happens to have.

But what are the negatives of your scheme requiring parental contributions? There are a few hurdles, but they are not insurmountable. Schools tend to be nervous about them as they are unused to asking for and processing the regular collection of money from families. The first three points below are covered in some detail in later sections, but we summarise them here for your executive convenience:

- Selling the scheme to parents. There is a substantial amount of effort that needs to be put into persuading parents that they should part with their money in the first place. After all, they pay taxes already don't they? The heading of this paragraph is a little provocative, but that's because the process is one of selling – not devices, but the educational vision that they will help deliver. Please see the section on Change Management with Parents for full details.

Consideration needs to be given to a sliding scale of contributions based on a family's ability to pay, which may be affected by several factors (usually FSM status and multiple siblings attending the school at the same time).

- Reaching financial and educational viability. As a rough guide, you need to achieve sign-up to the scheme in excess of 80% of the population, for two reasons;
  - o 20% of the cohort not having a personal device can just about be addressed through having enough school-owned devices to allow temporary borrowing. Remember, not every child will be using the device every lesson (let's assume 25% utilisation) so you will only need one school-owned device for every four pupils not taking part, approximately. In time, participation will rise as students and families understand that it's not going away and that there are important advantages in owning the device rather than accessing one from the common stock.
  - o 80% seems to be a tipping point at which 1-to-1 project have the momentum to carry staff forward with the change. Any less than this and it is, arguably, not worth planning lessons that have opportunities for device use. If they're not used in lessons, pupils will start to leave them at home, and the cycle accelerates. Pretty soon parents will stop paying (because they're not seeing the benefit educationally) and before you know it, the whole thing falls apart. The staff room cynic has been proved right, partially through their own passive resistance to change.

- Administering contributions. The next issue is the administration of these payments. The ideal is to have every parent set up a Direct Debit, but the reality is that many may not have a) an income reliable enough to guarantee the commitment will be met or b) a bank account. In our experience, it is necessary to offer, in a targeted and quiet manner, the option to pay in cash to those families that need to. If the numbers of such can be kept low, this isn't a huge burden.

- Dealing with debtors. Managing the payments month-on-month needs to be achieved in an affordable way. Many commercial providers will offer a 'parent portal' to do this but this is rarely value for money or particularly good. The alternative is for the school to administer these payments themselves. Please see Section 4.2.7.1 below for a more detailed analysis of these options.

- Funding the shortfall. With the best will in the world, there will be some contributions which just do not materialize, and yet the suppliers to whom you owe money will still send in their bills every quarter. This is the kind of thing that gives Business Managers sleepless nights. The best way to deal with this is to build in a contingency to your modelling (see below), collecting ever-so-slightly more than is necessary to break even and thereby guarding against drop-outs (people leaving the school) and bad debtors. If those with their hands on the purse strings are made aware of your judicious foresight early on, they tend to be a lot less worried about this aspect of risk.

4.2.6   The importance of a good financial model

All of the above is made much clearer and less scary once you have a good spreadsheet model for your project.

As any KS3 child will tell you, spreadsheet modelling is useful because it allows us to ask 'what if' questions and see what the financial impact of decisions would be on an overall project cost, without actually having to find out in real life.

The model will help you to finesse your scheme to get the per-month per-pupil cost down to a figure that you judge will be attractive or at least acceptable to parents. In contributory schemes with which the authors have been involved, it has felt quite crucial to get this number below £10.

If Excel is not your strong point, recruit the help of your friendly local Computer Studies, Business Studies or Maths teacher, or the school's Business Manager, for whom it almost certainly will be.

What does a good 1-to-1 financial model look like?

- It needs to be built around those variables that are most likely to change over the course of your planning and which will have the largest impact on the cost – namely the quantity and type of device.

- Include variables for case (£15-30) and insurance (£25-30) costs, these are fairly certain to be needed.

- It is sensible to include a small annual cost for app purchases (£10? The most expensive Apple apps that used to be chargeable are now free).

- It is helpful to separate out student devices and associated costs from those related to staff, as this will allow you to cleanly model the real-terms cost to families of equipping their child with a device without polluting this number with staff or infrastructure-related expenses. It is important at the marketing stage (if running a contributory scheme) to be able to demonstrate the cost effectiveness of what you are offering, compared to what they would pay in the shops.

- Before calculating the per-student costs, introduce another variable – the figure that the school will contribute from other sources of income (Pupil Premium, et cetera). This figure should be used to offset the direct cost to families of the things that make up the package (device, case, insurance, apps), rather than swallowed up in scheme costs more generally. In this way, you can clearly demonstrate how specific funding streams have been spent on pupils.

- These contribution costs should be surfaced as an overall package cost (e.g. £350) as well as per-month rentals and optional final payment. You will need the help of your leasing partner to get this bit right. Parents find this level of transparent detail very reassuring – they will want to know exactly and categorically what they are committing to.

- Remember that you are modelling the cost of leasing devices, not owning them, so don't include the Residual Value (the optional final payment) cost in the bottom line as this will never be paid by the school. Parents will want to see this, but staff devices only need to show the rental costs associated with them.

- A simple tweak to these contribution costs is to also include a +5% and +10% line, to see what you would need to charge parents in you wanted to build a little fat into the model. This could be to create a small contingency or to allow for a limited number of defaulted contributions.

- The model should have lines for every other infrastructural and background cost, the full extent of which may not become clear until you move through your diligence; the network cabling, switching, wireless, broadband, AV integration, joined-up systems, storage solutions, MDM.

- When totalling the whole-scheme costs, include lines that show overall cost to the school including and excluding VAT, so that there is no confusion over this later.

- It makes sense to operate to a 'worst case scenario', albeit moderated by what you know already, so that the school's leadership is fully aware of the possible cost. For example, even if you think a free MDM may be sufficient, budget for a paid one. From that point on, every frighteningly expensive possibility that doesn't materialize into a reality is a good news story and yet further evidence of your wisdom and prudence. Far better than the reverse!

If all this seems a bit complex, there is a good modelling tool, including up-to-date pricing on all the popular device types and the leasing figures you will need at www.educate1to1.org

The modelling tool lets you enter the variables that you know (such as number of devices) and prompts you to estimate those you might not (e.g. case cost), filling in all the blanks like current device pricing. That's fine as far as it goes - it gives you a good idea of the total capital cost of your project, but the really useful bit is the way the tool interacts with leasing rates, because it's actually these numbers that you need to know to judge affordability. You can also tweak some lease variables (how many years you want the lease to run, whether you want to front- or back-load the payments, how much of the school's money you want to put in, et cetera) and the model will produce monthly per-device per-pupil figures showing you how much the scheme costs in real terms.

There is no other way to do this without meeting with lots of lease companies and going through a protracted process of teasing out the costs in a meaningful format. The lease rates that drive the model have been provided by a lessor that we consider to be trustworthy, but there's no obligation to do anything other than anonymously play around with some 'what if' scenarios. The tool is there to use to get an idea of what you'd need to find (either from school funds or recovered from contributions) in order to make your 1-to-1 project sustainable.

4.2.7 Parent Portals

If you are running a contributory scheme, one of the headaches to overcome is the administration around parental sign-up and then managing their payments month by month. As an answer to these problems, many device suppliers offer Parent Portals to schools.

There are some major benefits to having an online portal;

- Marketing the project is simplified, with parents able to see online all the details of the programme, sign-up to take part, add payment details and make any choices that are needed

- It can also serve as a self-service portal for keeping their payment details up to date and for initiating insurance claims

- They promise to handle the chasing of defaulted/ failed payments

The biggest problem with portals is their ludicrous cost. These costs are always structured around a per-device per-month model. This is sold to schools quite disingenuously as 'As little as a £1 a month per child' (but the cost can be as high as £1.50 in our experience).

What the sales people never point out is that they are offering a product which costs the same to deliver to one set of parents as it does to a thousand, and yet their price scales up ridiculously. We're not being totally fair to the portal providers, as every transaction carries a banking charge, but it is pennies and doesn't justify the price point the market seems to have settled on. Take our 'average' school with a 1000 devices on a 3 year lease – that 36 monthly payments being made 1000 times. Even at the £1 rate, the cost to the school will be £36,000. At £1.50 that soars to £54,000.

To put even the £36k into context, it's more than the same school would pay to license all of its Microsoft products; every desktop OS, all its servers, every copy of Office on every computer, for the same three-year period.

It can even be hard to get suppliers to admit that this charge exists, so hidden is it within the package. To us this seems an inappropriate model that capitalizes on the hackneyed old marketing line of 'Only 5p per day!' and encourages schools to pass this inflated cost on to parents through the contributions they are making, not always knowingly. What would be much fairer would be a flat licence fee that reflects the true value of the service being offered; schools should probably pay a couple of thousand for the functionality described, but this wouldn't pay for the banks' transaction charges (which are a few pence a time). Having been through this at length with various portal providers, our advice is simple; the starting price of

£1.24 per device per month (or whatever they quote) is only a jumping-off point. You should be able to halve that, at least, through tough negotiation. And if they say it's free, or refuse to clarify the cost, you are probably not being given the full picture.

Be extremely cautious of portal providers that offer to be the first line contact for an insurance claim. Whilst having a company deal with insurance claims for you is useful, you always want the ability to go direct. You also need to keep an oversight of how many insurance claims are made, how many are rejected, etc. Many families will see your 1-to-1 scheme and everything associated with it as the school's issue to deal with and will arrive at reception demanding help to resolve disputes with the insurer (this is the most common issue). Without access to the insurer direct, you can't really do anything to help or placate angry parents.

The final problem with portals is that many promise to take away all the work, and all the risk, of managing payments and insurance claims but in reality, deliver a service that schools don't in practice find that helpful.

In the case of a missed payment, a generic email gets sent, followed by another one a few days later. For some portals, this is all that they do to chase money that's owed. The likelihood of these two emails resulting in a payment is low – we know of one school that is now chasing almost £40,000 of what will mostly become irrecoverable 'bad' debt. Please see the next section for a recommended model of payment management.

Still, some portals are better than others, and some are operated by more responsible companies. If you are considering using a portal, you should check any terms and conditions carefully to see what it is the provider actually commits to doing. One final thing to confirm is that they are not entitled to hold and make interest on parental contributions for extended periods of time, which has been known in the past. The money should come directly and immediately to the school so as not to give you any cash flow issues, or indeed to rob you of the interest it could be making in the school's bank account.

4.2.7.1 The alternative – administering payments yourself

This is far from impossible and shouldn't scare a well-organised school with a decent back-office team. The DIY approach also scores above outsourcing in one important respect (apart from the cost); at the end of the day it will be the school's responsibility to chase debt one way or another. If you are in control from the outset, this need not turn negative and formal.

Setting up payments to begin with doesn't require a clever online system, it can be managed through paper forms quite adequately. Direct Debit is preferable to Standing Order as it allows you to vary the amount taken, which might be useful in terms of catching up with missed payments and for the final, optional payment. Before you can collect Direct Debits, the school's bank will need to give its approval. BACS (who operate DD) have a simple guide to the set up process on their website: http://www.bacs.co.uk/Bacs/Businesses/DirectDebit/Collecting/Pages/GettingStarted.aspx

A good tip is to pre-populate these forms as far as possible using a spreadsheet of families and the mail-merge facility of Word. In this way you can remove many of the errors that might otherwise creep in, leaving parents to just supply their sort code, account number, bank address and signature. You will no doubt have reached this conclusion for yourself already, but it makes sense to have a master spreadsheet from the outset of your project which you use to track pupils' details - which device choice, payment method, any pertinent notes, etc.

The reference field is an important one to get right, as it is by this reference that you will be able to track the monthly payments. An intelligent reference choice might be something like '1to1*FamilyName_Initial*'.

Direct Debit forms will need careful checking for missing information before being sent to the parents' named banks. It is sensible to photocopy each form before sending them off. Any errors/ omissions identified by this process can be corrected face to face at the rollout events, though this does slow things down. It's best if these problems can be chased down beforehand.

The on-going collection of payments requires the partnership of the Finance and Pastoral teams. Firstly, someone needs to reconcile the list of who has paid this month's contributions with the list of who has signed up to the scheme, to identify anyone who has not paid. We cannot emphasize enough how important it is that this is done in a timely manner, every month.

The school's bank can supply monthly statements in a format compatible with Excel (.csv is most common). This allows you to quite easily do a gap-analysis once incoming payments have been sorted alphabetically by reference (remember the intelligent format you chose for this?). You don't need to type in *every* payment, just to identify the missing ones. Payments received can just be copied down the column.

Then the Pastoral team comes into play – no one is better suited to managing the delicate relationship with (typically) hard-to-reach families than those responsible for their child's welfare. It's easy to see from the spreadsheet who hasn't made a payment, and to pass this on to the HoY, Form teacher, etc. Relationships will already be in place, and agreeing how families will keep up their contributions is much more likely to succeed with someone they know than by paying a third-party firm with a payment portal to send automatically generated generic emails (which is generally all they'll do).

If you want to make a cold financial decision about which method – portal or self-administration – is best, you will need to take account not only of the portal's cost, but also of the lost revenue from failed collections which may result. Whatever solution you decide is right for your circumstances, early intervention by trusted school staff must play a part.

Section 4.3 Some important messages from our friends at HMRC

4.3.1   VAT

Let's begin by dispelling a myth - VAT, or Value Added Tax, is payable by all schools. Those who are maintained by the state are able to reclaim VAT through an annual process, but they are not exempt. This has several potential implications for your project.

Firstly please note that we are not tax advisors, so if in any doubt, schools should seek professional advice. In schemes of this scale, the 20% VAT payable on devices may present a substantial cash flow implication for your school as you will need to carry the cost of VAT (which could be £70k-£90k for a 1000 pupil school going fully 1-to-1) for up to a year. Your Business Manager/ Director of Finance needs to know about this burden, which may not be an issue at all – only they will know. For schools operating in deficit, this might be a significant problem.

Reclaiming the VAT, if your school is state maintained, is achieved through submission of an annual return to HMRC stating why VAT should be repaid. An important test applied to whether VAT can be reclaimed is that of equability; is the thing you're claiming on available to all students, rather than specific individuals. Let's use the example of a school going 1-to-1 with its Year 7 intake of 200 pupils. If they achieve an 80% take up on the scheme, that leaves 40 pupils without a device. However, buying 10 school-owned devices and making them available to non-participants as needed (on a ratio of 1:4, based on a realistic 25% utilization in lessons), 100% of the population has access to the item against which the school is reclaiming VAT. It's important to note that this 'population' could be class, a year or any group – it's not necessary to give the entire school access to something before the equability test can be demonstrated as met. Now all this may seem a byzantine technicality or an unnecessary hoop-jump. Your school's auditors would disagree. The last thing you want is to model excluding VAT (e.g. at 80% of the VAT-inclusive price) and then get a nasty and potentially scheme-derailing, career-stunting surprise when HMRC reject your attempt to reclaim this.

The final thing to understand about VAT is how it interacts with parental contribution schemes. It is really important that any such schemes do not appear to avoid the payment of VAT. To say that HMRC frown upon VAT avoidance something of a euphemism – far better to describe their countenance in such matters as the grim, unrelenting pursuit of offenders with the ferocious use of tax law and the threat of professional liability. You probably want to steer clear of that.

What would be deemed VAT avoidance? Most commonly it is where schools allow parents to pay 'up front' for a device on which the school intends to reclaim the VAT, without charging the parent for the VAT. In effect the school is retailing devices without paying the tax that retailers are liable for. However, if you ask parents for a regular contribution, followed by a final payment to transfer title to them, they are *operating* a device that the school owns and, quite legally and properly, has reclaimed the VAT against. The exception to this is the Residual Value payment, on which the VAT cannot be reclaimed, on current HMRC advice. The selection of a trustworthy leasing partner who has integrity and more than a passing knowledge of the Academies' Financial Handbook is therefore essential (see below).

4.3.2   Gift Aid

You will be aware of Gift Aid, as every time you sponsor someone for a charitable act these days, you are invited to tick a box declaring that you are a UK taxpayer and that your donation is therefore eligible to receive Gift Aid.

Gift Aid is a tax break for charities by which the government gives them back the basic rate of tax that you, the donor and taxpayer, have already paid through your salary deductions on the money that you're handing over. This currently amounts to 20%.

If your school is using a parental contribution approach, then this has benefits that we won't insult the reader by pointing out. However, it's a bit of a minefield and needs very careful consideration. Firstly, you are probably not eligible to claim Gift Aid – the exceptions will be independent schools (which are generally charities) and schools that are part of a chain which is operated by a charity. In these two cases, Gift Aid may be worth looking at, although in the case of independent schools it's unlikely (or at least ill-advised) that you'll be seeking parental contributions separately to fees. In the case of schools that are operated by a charity, then it is for your charity to decide if it thinks running a Gift Aid scheme is legal. Having looked at the law on this and taken advice, the professional opinion seems to be 'It depends on HMRC's interpretation of the scheme'. Still, the fact that schemes that do leverage Gift Aid already exist and HMRC are fully aware of them indicates that a well-informed and advised charity could proceed cautiously.

If your school is not a charity, there is a legal route to accessing Gift Aid but it is not necessarily the right choice for you; we suggest a careful reading of this section before seriously considering using a third-party charity to leverage Gift Aid.

There are some well known organisations that promise to help schools achieve affordable 1-to-1 schemes through the use of Gift Aid, and what they do is perfectly legal and above board, it's just not without its compromises and complications.

Here's how it works;

- They are a charity and as such are eligible for Gift Aid.

- You, the school, pay a membership fee to be part of their 'club'. This is usually annual and a few hundred pounds. In return, you get access to their expertise, briefings and their parental marketing materials. It's hard to quantify the value of this, but as you're reading this book, we're contractually obliged to say that you already have access to all of the expertise and materials you need.

- If you want to proceed with their scheme, there's a substantial fee — around 15% of the scheme value typically.

- You get parents to sign up to 'donate' and tick the Gift Aid box, and the additional 20% flows back from the government.

And here are the compromises;

- For Gift Aid to be applicable, the payment of the donation cannot be linked to the receipt of any goods or services, not even a voucher or lottery ticket. It has to be a no-strings donation. What this means for you is that *you are going to have to give every pupil a device, regardless of their parents' willingness or ability to make a donation.* With Gift Aid delivering a 20% benefit, you don't need to teach A Level statistics to work out that 80% of parents will have to agree to donate before this will break even. Please note that we have not included in these figures any charges levied by the organization running the Gift Aid scheme, which could make that 80% threshold much higher.

- Gift Aid can only be claimed on *donations*. This is a really important distinction from a parent's *contribution*. The language that you will have to very carefully use in your communications with parents has to be clear to point out that they're making a donation to assist with the affordability of the scheme, not in relation to getting a device. The two things have to be demonstrably separate. E.g. the school is running a 1-to-1 scheme that is going to cost £500k overall, including all the infrastructure and ancillary stuff that needs buying, with every pupil receiving their own device. Parents are asked to make a charitable donation to assist with the cost of this initiative.

The risks here are two-fold; firstly, some parents may take the view that as they get the goods regardless of whether they donate, the pragmatic thing to do is to not donate. Those that have donated may well suspect that many others haven't, and feel resentment or worse — stop paying. Secondly, as it's a donation, the school has a much weaker hold over the parents should they default. For example, in the case of straight-forward contribution, you can get parents to sign up to an agreement, including a clear description of what the school will do in the case of payments stopping (e.g. reclaiming the device). This is much harder to enforce, and potentially in breach of the law around Gift Aid, in the case of a donation scheme.

- Gift Aid is only applicable to the donations on UK taxpayers. Not all of your parents will fall into this category and, for schools serving challenging demographics, this will be even more of an issue.

When does a Gift Aid scheme make sense? The answer, to me, seems to be quite a mathematical value for money one:

A. when a school is already committed to giving every child a device regardless of their ability to pay, **and;**
B. when the school is confident that the donations they can collect, minus the admin costs due to the scheme's operators, will exceed 80% of the total cost of supplying the devices **or;**
C. the school is part of a charitable trust which can operate its own Gift Aid collection and avoid the fees of a third-party scheme, lowering the donation sign-up break-even point to a straight 80%

A) is a deal-breaker, and either B) or C) must be true.

Certainly something to approach with your eyes open to the compromises as well as the benefits.

Section 4.3 The importance of the right insurance

As indicated elsewhere in this chapter, the market for mobile device insurance is an odd one, and also one that seems to be developing very rapidly as the insurance industry comes to grips with the spread of 1-to-1 projects throughout the education sector.

The first remarkable thing about the market is how under-crowded it is, despite appearances to the contrary. It was only when one takes the time to compare in detail the T&Cs of the six or seven insurance policies being offered by various device suppliers that it is discovered that despite a multitude of different trading names, there are only actually a couple of insurers operating in this space. A third has recently entered the market. There may be others, but they're certainly not being extensively resold by the people who do 95% of the business with schools.

This is far from ideal because where there is limited competition, it tends to follow that prices go up rather than down and the Terms and Conditions remain harsh. Without competition from several providers, there's no incentive to improve the deal to attract more customers. This will undoubtedly improve as the customer base expands, but at the moment your choice is limited. That's not to say that negotiation of terms is impossible (see below).

The next thing of note is that there are two distinct strata of insurance products being sold to schools. We'll call the first one the 'Adequate' stratum and the second the 'Downright Useless' one. We'll go into a bit of detail about the things you need in an adequate mobile device insurance policy a bit further on and just point out here that currently many schools are effectively uninsured, such is the poverty of the cover provided by the product for which they are paying £10-20 per-device per-year.

The final thing that makes this market 'interesting' is its volatility. In 2012, an adequate policy cost around £16. By 2014 this had risen to between £20-25. We will not be at all surprised if they breach the £30 mark by the middle of 2015. At the same time, insurers have been tightening the terms of the their product, making it harder to claim, in effect.

The reason for both of these changes is simply that the industry was fairly naïve about school insurance in the early days, possibly failing to understand that whilst it was the school (with its strong credit reference, solid income and low historic rate of claims) that was buying the insurance, the device was being operated and, to all intents and purposes owned by a child. Sometimes that child used it as a computer. Other times it became a makeshift goal post. Amazingly, every time a new iPad was announced, insurance claims would rocket as a whole generation of new consumers was introduced to the wonders of insurance fraud. Allegedly.

It's safe to say that the insurance industry has now woken up to the elevated risk, and policies are priced and written to match. Unfortunately, just like the cost of your car insurance, it's the profligacy of other drivers that is to blame. Perhaps it will even out soon – to be fair, the early adopter schools whose sometimes staggering loss rates have led to this price inflation did not benefit from recent developments, such as kill switches making tablets less attractive to thieves, or MDM systems that made locking down and tracking down a device much more robust.

The point we are, slowly, building up to here is that despite the cost, lack of choice and worryingly weak cover offered by some policies, it is vital that your devices are adequately insured;

- Firstly, your lessor will insist upon it. They may even specify the level of cover that is required. This is because they need to be able to sell it after it's spent three years being slung around in a school bag.

- Secondly, loss and damage do occur, and more often than those promoting 1-to-1 to schools would have you believe. Admittedly, it's rare for devices to be stolen in school or taken on the street with the threat of violence, but children are forgetful and these things are mobile, that's kind of the point. Damage is by far the greatest reason to insure though. Most devices are a beautiful synergy of glass and aluminium, designed to look good on a coffee table; the classroom and playground are rather more robust environments generally, and cracked screens are a frequent occurrence.

What should you look for in an adequate insurance policy then?

- A limited and acceptable set of circumstances under which a claim won't be honoured – these are called 'exclusions'. Ones to watch out for are screen damage (this exclusion of which makes your policy virtually useless) and water ingress (an occasional problem due to rain on the walk home/ water bottles in bags). On the screen damage point, accidental damage should definitely be covered, with no demand of proof (which would be impossible in the absence of CCTV footage). Acts of God and Force Majeure are always in there for entertainment value; your insurance probably won't pay out in the event of a nuclear winter or a plague of frogs.

- An exclusion you probably won't ever get away from is 'Unattended Theft', sometimes just referred to as loss. This means leaving it in plain sight, like on a park bench or a bus seat and walking off. The theft clauses also often exclude thefts where no sign of a crime is found, and for which a police crime number cannot be obtained, such as theft from a bag in the changing rooms or from a drawer in an unlocked room.

- Some inadequate policies also exclude thefts where no threat of force was used, e.g. bag snatching or sneak theft, rather than a confrontational mugging – this is particularly problematic for schools in inner city contexts. The level of proof demanded of a genuine theft can vary too, but a police report is normally what is asked for. Similarly, thefts where inadequate security provisions were made by the owner (e.g. it was left on the dashboard of your car, or on a table next to an open ground-floor window) can be the cause of rejected claims.

- Check that parents can initiate and manage their own claims even though the school is the named insured party. If not, you may be letting yourself in for a substantial and unwelcome administrative workload.

- Excess clauses attempt to disincentivise claims by making the claimant pay the first £50/£100/£150 of the damage or replacement cost. Whilst this is an accepted feature of car and home insurance policies, the parents we've discussed this with have been very clear about their expectations of the school-provided policy having a 'zero excess'. However, an excess is a very effective way to reduce your premiums, to have parents encourage their child to take care of the device and to disincentivise fraud. Schools in challenging contexts may want to use this lever to shape behaviour, if you think it can be enforced. Our advice if you are considering having an excess on the policy is to consult with parents and publicise its existence from the off. Don't let them discover it for themselves when attempting to claim!

- Another method insurance companies use to reduce claims is limiting them to one per year per device. This could unfairly punish the unlucky, as well as fairly restrict the fraudulent, so as with the excess point, consult and publicise widely if you are going to use a policy with this restriction. The appetite of parents is definitely for a 'no quibble' policy, but this may be only our limited experience.

- Most policies will insist the device is in a case, if it's a tablet. Some go further and state that the case should have four hard corners and a screen cover. Some demand that the insurer needs to approve your choice of case. Some go even further and name a specific case that must be used. As case choice is routinely the single facet of the whole project that gets schools and pupils most exercised (we are being serious), we find it hard to imagine that this last point would be acceptable. The children are going to want a case that looks good, not some rubberized military grade behemoth that weighs as much as the tablet and doubles its size.

  A final point on cases; choosing an insubstantial - though insurer-approved - one may seem like a canny saving, but that won't stop the same insurer raising your premiums next year if the poor protection offered by the case is resulting in lots of claims. This could end up as a false economy.

Unfortunately, the only way to be certain that you have the right product for your needs is to read the T&Cs in detail. They can be quite long and you'll definitely need your magnifying glass. However, be reassured that having read the list above, it will at least all make sense to you.

As with anything in life, an insurance deal of the scale you'll be entering into should be negotiable. For our 'average' 1-to-1 school we're talking about £75,000 in premiums over three years, in today's prices. This negotiation won't be simple, and getting it started is the hardest part. To do this requires direct access to the insurer, which often won't be possible if you're buying it as part of a package from a device supplier.

The insurer will resolutely tell you these are their 'Standard T&Cs', to which you will reply, with irresistible logic, that their very use of the term 'Standard' creates (indeed requires) the existence of 'Non-standard T&Cs' too, and it is these that you wish to discuss.

Furthermore, and this will depend on the attitude of the insurer, but if a school can provide evidence of why it is a lower risk than average (perhaps you are high achieving, with a low rate of exclusions or an Outstanding Ofsted judgment for behaviour? Or maybe your intake is single-sex and highly selective?), then it should be possible to further reduce the cost and soften certain clauses.

One final point - GAP Insurance. This is a separate policy that covers the gap between what your mobile device insurance will pay out and the full value of the device. If you have a good insurance policy as described above, this will only be the VAT (which you may be able to reclaim, if your school is maintained by the state). Device suppliers love to sell GAP insurance, but we're far from convinced of its value to schools.

4.3.1   Managing insurance claims

It is doubtful that you want to be the conduit for all insurance claims – this is an administrative burden that is best passed to parents. If you are using a parent portal, this is the obvious route for the process to begin. If not, use a page of your 1-to-1 marketing website to summarise the insurance terms, link to the full T&Cs and provide the insurer's phone number for the initiation of claims.

Regardless of whether you use a parent portal of handle things yourself, you will want to maintain an oversight of the insurance situation as your scheme progresses. This is for many reasons;

- As noted in the leasing section below, you will need to advise the lessor of any new serial numbers replacing old when a device is lost/ damaged beyond economic repair and is therefore replaced by the insurer.

- It is in your interest to suppress the number of insurance claims wherever possible, through enforcing behaviours (such as not using devices while walking around, for example) and reminding pupils regularly about the need to take care. Another important action is to educate pupils about the terms of the insurance through assemblies, to avoid attempts at fraudulent claims which would never actually be honoured (such as non-existent muggings). You want to take these steps because your loss rate will affect future premiums. Some schools have found themselves to be uninsurable in Years 2 and 3 following unrestrained levels of loss in Year 1.

Some insurers provide their own, free insurance portal to allow parents to enter claims and schools to oversee them - this is quite a useful value-added extra.

To make sure that you can stay informed and in control, have a nominated member of support staff maintain the relationship with the insurance provider and request regular reports of claims submitted by families. Even better, if you are using an insurance portal, access this information yourself. This may help you to pro-actively intervene if you suspect fraud and help pupils to find 'lost' devices rather than attempt to get a replacement.

Section 4.4 A formula for commercial effectiveness

This section aims to equip the reader with the things we've learned over several years on both sides of the fence – both as school leaders and (in the case of one of the authors) as a procurement consultant in the educational technology sector.

There has always been a healthy skepticism in schools about companies trying to do business with them, at times bordering on suspicion. It's natural for people working in public sector/ not-for-profit organisations to feel a little suspicious of those trying to make money from them. This is a useful attitude to have and we suggest you cultivate and nurture it.

What is a less useful characteristic of schools, however, is a lack of commercial awareness. This is unsurprising – they're run by people who have risen largely due to their teaching ability and people management skills, not by former bankers or accountants.

However, this can be quite a weakness when entering the murky waters of large-scale technology procurement and leasing. When you consider that we are talking about contracts that will stretch into the hundreds of thousands of pounds, even minor missteps can have far reaching and expensive consequences. You are almost certainly going to be asking parents to help finance your 1-to-1 project, and for this reason alone there is a moral imperative to get the cost down as low as possible. Just as importantly, the cheaper you can make it, the higher the take up will be by families, the greater the momentum created in school, and the more likely that the change will succeed.

The most common pitfall is that of *credulity*. Too often, schools get into commercial relationships with people that they like or feel a cultural fit with or, in the worst cases, those who they meet first, rather than companies that have been diligently assessed for their performance, stability, integrity and value for money. We know, because we've done so ourselves. The main reasons for this are a lack of time to fully assess the market and a lack of experience in sorting the best companies and proposals from the rest. Cultural fit is indeed an important criterion when selecting a partner with whom you may work for a number of years, it's just not the only one and, arguably, not the most important.

So, when preparing for what will probably be the biggest purchasing decision of your professional life to date, you should definitely involve the school's Business Manager/ Director of Finance/ Bursar fully, and from Day One. The scale and complexity of a 1-to-1 procurement are not something to be juggled with a teaching timetable or handled by someone who, with respect, does not have the requisite experience. Ask for help – you'll be glad of the sharing of the workload and won't have to convince the people who sign the Purchase Orders that the proposal you're accepting represents best value later on.

Hopefully we've gone some way to convincing you that this isn't something you should be handling in your Friday free period - what follows is a tried and tested formula for getting the best commercial deal to ensure your 1-to-1 project can be delivered for as little as possible, sustained beyond and initial wave and, ultimately, become a success.

4.4.1 Disaggregate

Probably the worst thing you can possibly do is buy a solution off-the-shelf, pre-packaged by a '1-to-1 provider'.

There are lots and lots of companies hovering around the 1-to-1 space and they have all helpfully put together ready-made packages for the convenience of the busy school leader. "Why visit several shops", the argument runs, "when our supermarket has everything you need under one roof and, what's more, we're the experts who can guide you through your every requirement. You need an upgraded wireless system you say? Please step this way Sir. Careful - some of aisles are full of confusing, hard to reach stuff that you really won't understand. Just say 'yes' and we'll take care of everything".

Where the analogy fails though is that supermarkets are transparently comparable (there are websites and apps devoted to price checking) and in reality, you don't just turn up and let someone else fill your trolley, you pick and choose the products you want, making hundreds of tiny best-value and quality driven decisions along the way.

What this 'one-stop-shop' offer hides, of course, are numerous small margins from which profit can be derived. Every time a product or service intersects with your single supplier, there's a referral fee or a profit share in place. This isn't wrong, it's totally normal commercial practice. What is wrong is the way that these packages are marketed to schools ill equipped to challenge them.

It also encourages less than ethical behaviour from incumbent suppliers as the relationship matures. If they're supplying everything and are, in effect, the trusted advisor, there's little incentive to price keenly or to suggest products that may be better, cheaper or more suitable, yet with whom they do not have a juicy commercial arrangement.

So, **the single and simplest thing you can do that will save you the greatest amount of money is to disaggregate** – pull apart the packaged-up solutions and buy the constituents one at a time, and from different places.

There is additional effort in this, don't get us wrong – the price of this saving is the extra work you need to put in, but it is well worth it. Even if you only disaggregate the largest components of your project (those being the devices and the leasing), there is a huge economy to be made. Having carried out similar exercises in 2013 and 2014 and benchmarked the difference, the saving achieved was 14.6%. For context, 14.6% of the 'average' school's £500,000 project cost is £73,000. That's £73 per pupil, or just over £2 off their monthly contribution.

How to do this though?

4.4.1.1 Start with the money

Identify the leasing partner first, for two good reasons. You'll be able, with them, to build a financial model using their rates for use in later stages of the procurement and, most importantly, you'll have gained a trusted and knowledgeable commercial advisor.

Most of the time, leasing companies don't get to work 'client side' as they are always introduced by the package provider (which is usually some sort of device supplier), via a referral fee, naturally. This means they are under obligation through this commercial relationship. They're not going to tell you anything the introducer doesn't want you to hear.

If you identify your own lease provider, in isolation from any other part of the solution, and agree separately how the lease will be structured, what its terms are and how much it costs, they effectively work for you (see Section 4.5.2.2 below for detail on how to achieve this). They'll share, in confidence, their knowledge of the market and the players in it. Best of all, the money that they otherwise would have had to hand over to the solution provider can be negotiated off their price.

4.4.1.2 Have separate conversations: Device suppliers

Finding the right supplier for your device of choice should not be hurried. It is *the* critical commercial relationship that you need to get right as, even if you disaggregate multiple products and use several suppliers, the people who sell you the devices themselves will be an on-going source of news, knowledge, training and experience around the implementation issues that you will face.

An intelligent first principle is not to meet with people who come knocking at your door. Would you even buy a tea towel in that way? Put yourself in control of the relationship from the off by identifying three or four potential companies you want to talk to. One good way to do this is by visiting other schools in your region who are one or two years ahead of you in their 1-to-1 project. They will have unambiguous views about who they are working with.

This can be a little anecdotal, however, so triangulate with a second data source: every major manufacturer and Operating System developer has an employee, or many of them, whose job it is to develop business in the education sector. Apple has regional people, as do Microsoft. Google (who develop the Android OS), and Toshiba and Samsung (who make the majority of Chromebooks and Android tablets used in schools) have someone in a national role currently. None of them work for the retailers of their products, so their job is not to sell you stuff (well, not in practical terms – think of them as marketing folk). They're primarily keen that you have a positive experience with their brand. If you already know the type of device you are after, get in touch with the right person from the list above and ask for supplier recommendations and reference sites.

There are some strict laws about spending large amounts of public money within the European Union which you've probably not come across before. This isn't the place or the manner in which to instruct you in how to run a competitive procurement, which is a specialized task due to complex EU law, would take the rest of the book and almost certainly prompt a strong desire to go and see what's on the telly. You probably don't need to worry about EU procurement law in this case because a) the value of the things you're actually buying with the public's money may not exceed the €207k threshold for each project and b) the big money that you're spending on several hundred devices is likely to be leased, so you are not in fact the purchaser, the lease company is. In that case you should check that your lessor has access to an EU compliant procurement framework. They will be best placed to advise you about the technicalities of what constitutes 'the project' and whether the rules of aggregation apply. Should either case a) or case b) above not be true, then you should seek specialist procurement support to stay the right side of the law

Here are some common sense, quick and easy steps to take to run a mock-procurement to access that bid pricing and establish the educational bone fides of the bidders:

- When negotiating with suppliers, you are not in fact offering to enter into contract with them, you are seeking 'bid pricing' and the opportunity to add the right partner into the supply chain you're putting together. It's your lessor who will eventually buy the devices.

- When you have a shortlist of companies you would consider working with (and keep it short, as the effort of bid scoring is considerable; 4-6 companies at most), draw up a document describing your requirements, which will include supply of devices but may also cover other services as well.

- Describe the context of your project so that bidders know the scale of the opportunity. Talk also about your school's educational values and challenges. Remember, you want to check that these people understand your context and education more generally.

- Tell them your scoring criteria – this can be as simple as how many/ what percentage of the marks will be awarded for price, value added, educational experience, local presence, cultural fit, et cetera. For each criterion, you need to ask at least one question.

- One thing to be sure to include is a request that they detail what their Added Value will be. Often this will run to free services or training; whether they are actually free will be revealed in their overall pricing.

- Include a spreadsheet for them to fill in and insist that they don't alter the format. This will afford you the ability to make 'apples with apples' comparisons between bidders.

- Give the selected companies a limited window of response and tell them that this is a competitive process to identify your long-term partner.

- Make it clear that you do not want to talk to them about leasing as you already have a leasing partner in place. You may be surprised at how firm you have to be on this point – well, you would be if you didn't already know quite how much profit is hidden in this relationship.

- When their bids are returned, score them against the criteria you decided on. This can be quite laborious, so have colleagues take separate sections that match their experience or interest and ask them to score that section of every bid. This also has the advantage of making the judgment more even.

- Meet with a sub-set of bidders (or all of them – but you'll probably rule some out right off the bat) to go through questions arising from their submission and, more importantly, to meet the actual person you'll be working with. We are constantly surprised by how often a strong 'on paper' bid is utterly undermined by the quality of the people who will be delivering, and vice versa. In short, it's always worth meeting with potential partners face to face.

- This is also the fun part, the bit where you get to give them a gentle but persistent kicking over their price. Some of the negotiating tips in Section 4.5.5 below apply equally to this conversation.

- An additional, and pretty sneaky tactic is to ask suppliers to quote for a bunch of stuff like storage lockers and don't really challenge them on the cost of these. At the same time, push them hard on device cost. Standard operating procedure is to push profit into certain products and make the customer's priority your loss leader. However, you can subvert this by only buying the devices at the price you have agreed and getting your lockers or whatever elsewhere (if you ever genuinely needed them in the first place). Like we say; sneaky.
- Finally, when you've got the price you want from the partner of choice, introduce your leasing company into the equation, feed the agreed bid pricing into your financial model and start to plan the various waves of deployment (which will probably be structured into separate lease schedules).

4.4.1.3 Have separate conversations: Infrastructure providers

Wired and wireless infrastructure can be a major outlay, perhaps reaching £100-200k in complex schools starting from a low base. Any procurement of that scale will see enormous variations between bids, as much as 30% in our experience. Why would you let someone else pick the supplier for you and then layer their management fee on top? The keenest prices and best implementation are also often found from smaller, more local companies. If you're in the situation of needing to upgrade cables, switches or wireless, take the time to run a separate, competitive procurement process, by which we don't mean ringing round for three quotes. If it's public money you're spending, do bear in mind the €207k EU threshold – that's around £172,500 currently.

4.4.1.4 Have separate conversations: Insurers

The market for Mobile Device Insurance is curious and confusing, and also changing rapidly at the moment as the insurance industry wakes up to the elevated risk that school 1-to-1 deployments have over more traditional environments. This is picked apart in detail in Section 4.3, but suffice to say that as insurance is usually bundled by device suppliers into their overall package, the terms and conditions vary wildly, as do the prices. If you have the capacity, it's a good idea to disaggregate this product too.

4.4.1.5 Revisit your choice of device partner at least every two years

Whilst having a known supplier that you trust and with whom you have invested time developing a relationship has a value all of its own, it makes sense to keep them on their toes and prevent prices from drifting up or, more likely, price cuts not being passed on. For this reason, re-run the procurement exercise after a decent interval, if only to keep them honest.

Annually, ideally, but bi-annually if you can't justify the time, tell them that you are going to benchmark their pricing by going back to the market. In order to *really* get them worried, tell them that whilst you truly value their partnership, et cetera, you're being pushed irresistibly hard by your governors/ sponsor to deliver efficiency savings and that you may be forced to go with the lowest price bidder. This should trigger the response you need; remember that it's ten times more expensive to win a new customer than retain an existing one – they'll be motivated to do what it takes to at least match what others are offering. You don't necessarily have to go into the same depth as you did the first time round unless you are unhappy with your supplier. The object is to sow fear and confusion and thereby force prices down, not to give yourself another bunch of bids to score.

4.4.2 Aggregate

Having just successfully divided and conquered by refusing to be sold an over-priced 'solution', the title of this section may seem a little counter-intuitive. The aggregation referred to here is of scale – accumulating greater numbers by which to drive down prices, by working with other schools.

If you can find other schools who want to buy similar things (and tablets are pretty similar) on similar timescales, then by aggregating your numbers you increase the opportunity size and hence your attractiveness to suppliers. In this manner, further price reductions on devices can be achieved, probably up to another 3% if you can attach several schools together. Suppliers will tell you repeatedly that the margins they operate on are slim, but their price breaks from manufacturers also operate on a sliding scale of 'transaction rebates' as well as volume bonuses, so the savings are certainly there to be made. There is also the caché of market share to bear in mind – there is value to them in being a leading supplier, so companies will want to gain additional schools on their books. Lastly, you can remind bidders that the addition of multiple new customers with only a single bid effort is highly efficient for them.

The challenges to putting together aggregated procurements are largely cultural – it can be difficult to convince a school that they're better off working with others. There's a fierce streak of independence running throughout the sector that, in procurement particularly, does it no favours. However, these challenges can be resolved by identifying similarities between schools and then demonstrating the benefits. The most important similarities needed are;

- Device brand (model is less important, as long as a single supplier can deliver everyone's requirements)

- Implementation timeline (but only in terms of years, not months)

- Region (as schools want to be able to rely on reasonably local service and support)

Once similar schools are found, what happens next is a repeat of the mock-procurement to leverage bid-pricing that is described above, just on a grander scale. Beyond the pricing advantage all the schools will gain, there is also the fact that when lots of schools are involved, your collective capacity to carry out the detailed scrutiny of bidders is also increased. The work gets easier, and the prices get lower.

For example, let's say five schools in the Midlands are all implementing some form of iPad 1-to-1 in 2014-2016, with a total need for 3700 devices over those two years. They agree together what their minimum requirements are, leaving aside things that are peculiar to individual schools and just concentrating on what they have in common. They draw up a bid document that asks for pricing on three different models of iPad. They exclude insurance and cases when it becomes clear that they all have different ideas about what they need. Still, they broadly hint at 'other associated goods and services' in their document, to keep bidders keen on the on-going opportunity.

The consortium approaches four suppliers with a regional presence and get three bids returned. After meeting will all three, it's obvious to the representatives of all the schools which supplier is offering the most, but they're not satisfied on the device prices. One school takes the lead in negotiating on the others' behalf and after a few days' to-ing and fro-ing via email and phone, they get their preferred supplier to better the price of all the other bidders. The schools individually send the supplier a Letter of Intent, giving a non-contractual assurance that they'll place their orders with the chosen supplier, based on the agreed pricing. The schools then carry on independently, as if they'd achieved this bid pricing on their own.

The really hard part is putting together your 'consortium' of schools in the first place. How do you go about finding schools on a similar path to your own? Previously, schools have had to rely on local knowledge and serendipitous connections they've made at conferences, or pay to participate in a formal buying consortium, such as those operated by groups of LAs.

There has to date been no other tool which matches schools with each other and allows them to aggregate their requirements based on common factors, which is why we've created one at www.educate1to1.org. It's free to use and has no strings attached - if you try it and it's not for you, that's fine. Even taking £5 off the cost of a device is, in the quantities we're talking about, going to make a significant difference to the schools, and the families involved. The online tool lets you identify others on a similar pathway and timeline and to work with them to get a better price for everyone.

Section 4.5 To buy or to lease?

4.5.1 Why buying is not the best idea

For most schools, this decision is an easy one, as they don't have a spare £300k laying around waiting to be spent. However, it is appealing to teachers' innate sense of thriftiness to try to buy rather than borrow. This is understandable, we have after all been raised to husband our resources – all

30 pairs of scissors are counted back in and that tiny stub of purple chalk is retained just in case something needs underlining. This is an unhelpful impulse in the case of 1-to-1 technology though, which is fast changing, constantly getting cheaper and has a limited shelf life.

Firstly there's the question of the capital and cash flow. One of the major positive shifts enabled by the 1-to-1 model is that of the move away from institutional towards personal ownership of devices. Over the lifetime of a mature 1-to-1 programme (let's say six years), the ambition *has* to be to culture the users into accepting that they should supply the hardware and the school should supply the connectivity, as this is the only way to break the cycle of budget-busting hardware refreshes every few years and concentrate school capital on other things. Buying the devices outright disincentivises schools from developing smoother cash flows, without enormous peaks on every refresh event. Schools are funded in a relatively smooth way (variations year to year are minor), so spending should follow the same pattern to avoid affordability-driven decisions.

Secondly is how much sense ownership makes full stop under the 1-to-1 model. When the time finally comes, you won't necessarily *want* to own a three-year old tablet that has had one almost-careful owner. Why not?

- The chances are its battery will be shot following 1000+ recharging cycles. This is a pretty good rule of thumb for mobile devices using current battery technology.

- It will probably only have 1 more year before it becomes obsolete in software terms. The original iPad, for example, was released in 2010 and was not capable of running iOS6, which was released just two and a half years later. Likewise, the iPhone 4S (release date: Autumn 2011) runs iOS8 (release date: Autumn 2014) with all the agility and poise of an arthritic hedgehog.

- Even reasonable wear and tear of a tablet over this length of time is likely to leave it in a distinctly 'foxed' rather than 'mint' condition, to borrow an analogy from the school librarian.

- There are pretty strict rules about how a school can dispose of assets purchased with public money. Any transfer of an asset (say an iPad owned by the school, to a parent) must represent value for money to the school. This is another auditor's tripwire that schools need to know about. Do you know what a Samsung Tab 4 will be worth in three years? You'd need to have a fair idea, as parents will want to understand before signing up how much you'll be asking them to pay at the end (see the section above on VAT for reasons why this is necessary).

- In summary, if you buy outright, you may be left with a large number of devices from which you can derive limited educational or financial benefit.

4.5.2 Why leasing is a good idea

The alternative is to lease. But the school sector has a vestigial fear of leasing, and not without reason, as many have had their fingers burned in the past by unscrupulous companies charging many times the value of the equipment being leased. In almost all those famous cases from the past three decades, the main culprit has been the person who signed without reading the contract, but we'll come back to the ways to pick a good lessor later in this chapter. For now, let's concentrate on **why leasing your 1-to-1 devices is a good idea**.

Firstly, some terms to understand: the company lending the money is known as the *lessor* and the school borrowing the money is the *lessee*. The thing being leased is referred to as the *asset*. Payments fall into two categories, *rentals*, which are the sums you pay during the lease on a monthly, quarterly or annual basis and *residual value* (often shortened to RV), which is the payment at the end of the lease, if you want to offer ownership of the asset to a third party (such as a parent).

So why should you almost certainly lease rather than buy?

- A well-negotiated operating lease can cost significantly less over two or three years than buying outright – up to 10% cheaper depending on how it is structured.

- The total cost of the project can be annualized, meaning that the cash flow smoothing described above is achieved and the project is more sustainable.

- The assets are the property of the lessor rather than the lessee, which simplifies things like what to do with devices that parents don't want to own at the end (answer: you just send them back to the lessor). If you've ever owned a car outright and had to sell it, you'll understand why this is a good thing.

- It is a reliable and legal way to offer parents the right to take ownership of the device at the end of the lease period – but it remains optional. This has benefits that merit discussion;

The option to own is important when selling the scheme because parents feel that they should get something back for the money they are investing, beyond the obvious benefit of operating the device for the duration of the lease. However, it's the *option* to own that seems to be important, rather than the actual exercising of this right; it's a psychological benefit which is rarely translated into making the final payment and taking title. Just like the school, when it comes down to it, the parents don't actually want to own a three-year old device, they want a new one. But they might not sign up in the first place without the sense of 'value for money' that this confers.

This is actually quite useful – it allows the school to placate parents' fears that they're just paying to hire the device, whilst also letting you present costs in a way that separates out monthly contributions from the RV payment, demonstrating how cheap it is to take part in the scheme if they choose not to own at the end.

4.5.2.1 How do lessors make their money?

So, if a three-year lease costs a school significantly less than the value of the asset, how do lessors make their profit? In some cases, they make it by charging the lessee quite a lot for the money they're borrowing (see below for tips on how to establish this), but an ethical lease works like this:

- You identify the assets you want to operate and the company you want to buy them from. Let's use the example of 1000 Chromebooks, which might retail at £170 each excluding VAT.

- You negotiate with the device supplier. Let's say through a combination of scale, charm and persistence you get the ex-VAT price down to £150. This means you'd need to borrow £150,000 to fund their outright purchase.

- Assuming you've agreed the terms of operation with the lessor (as usual, see below), they buy the assets at the price you've agreed with the device supplier, and the Chromebooks are delivered direct to the school.

- The lessor will charge the first rental payment immediately and then the rest of them at whatever interval you've agreed. In total these payments should add up to less than 100% of the £150,000 – probably somewhere below 95%, or around £47,000 per year.

- You operate the assets for the duration of the lease, abiding by any terms set (looking after them, not committing crimes with them, et cetera).
- Towards the end of the lease you offer parents the chance to exercise their option to buy, and collect the money from those who take it up.

- When the lease ends, you:
    - o Pay for any devices parents have decided to buy **and**;
    - o Return the remaining devices and walk away from the lease without further obligation, **or**;

- o Return the remaining devices and begin a new lease with new assets (in the case of an on-going 1-to-1 programme) **or**;
- o Negotiate the re-leasing of the existing assets (which we doubt you'll want to do).

- The lessor then makes the majority of their profit from the money you've collected from parents who want to take title (usually around 20% of the original value) or by selling the assets into emerging markets in the 2nd World.

So, you can see that for the school this isn't an effective method of *buying* devices (that would constitute a financing lease anyway, which state schools are not permitted to enter into), as the total cost is around 115-120% of the assets' value.

It is, however, a very cost-effective method of *operating* devices, as the total cost over three years will be lower than the cost of buying and, for the reasons we've explained above, after three years it really makes little sense to own the devices anyway.

4.5.2.2. *How to identify a scrupulous lessor*

Whilst we would hesitate to suggest that any company has anything other than your school's best interests at heart, it remains true that the objectives of commercial organisations may not be precisely aligned with those of an educational institution. In short, they're in it to make money and it's worth keeping that at the forefront of your mind. Oceanic naturalists can appreciate the beauty, poise and equal right to exist of the Great White, but that doesn't mean they don't use a shark cage and a very big harpoon gun…

Here are the things we've learned from going through the process several times:

There are good lessors and there are bad lessors, it's a bit like estate agents in that respect, except that the suits tend to be less shiny. Whilst they all wish to make a profit, some see this in very short terms, and others prefer to make it through lower margins and repeat custom. This will become obvious through the course of your negotiations and it goes without saying which of the two types you'll want to work with.

It's important that you understand the law around maintained schools leasing, because non-compliancy has serious implications for you, and there are some lessors who will offer non-compliant leases (because its easier to make money by bending the rules).

The Academies Financial Handbook deems both finance leases and hire purchase/ lease purchase products as a form of borrowing – Local Authority schools/ academies cannot enter this type of agreement. These schools can only take out an **operating lease**, which is strictly renting equipment for a period of time and therefore no money is borrowed. This is the only type of agreement a Local Authority school or an academy may enter. If a lessor tells you different, they are lying and have just given you a handy window on their ethics.

The maximum term for any operating lease must be three years. This can only be extended by request to the Secretary of State for Education. We can't imagine this actually gets as far as the SoS's desk, but for anything longer to be approved, there would need to be a really compelling reason. It's hard to think of many circumstances where lessors would want a longer term, if they are acting compliantly, as they need to recover their costs by selling the assets at the end of the term, and they'll be worth far more after three years than after four or five. That is unless they have already made their profit through the rental payments, which is not legal.

This is because the sum of the rentals that the school pays should always be less than the original capital value. If they are not, then you have a finance lease, plain and simple. The way this is assured is that the lease must demonstrate a present value of 89.9% prior to interest being added – e.g. the lessor must invest an absolute minimum of 10.1% Residual Value. Thus you can see that interest on rentals should be minimal, with the lessor gaining back their 10.1% investment by selling the asset at the end of the lease.

A Local Authority school or academy may never automatically own the equipment at the end of a lease – this includes pre arranged buy out prices – as this would make the agreement a lease purchase and therefore non-compliant. Where it is absolutely required (e.g. where you need to tell parents signing up to a scheme what they will have to pay at the end), a buy out price may be offered to a non-related third party. It must however be noted that this option is strictly not open to the school.

Full transparency of costs is a principle from which you should not allow yourself to be swayed. Explain that you need to see their full costs detailed in your spreadsheet model rather than their preferred format, which will allow more accurate comparison. This spreadsheet should show exactly how much would be payable at each stage and where the lessor is making their money. After all, there can only be one credible reason for hiding this from you, and that is because there's a cost being hidden too.

Any business that is offering this kind of service to schools should have a track record that can be researched and referenced as well as a trading history of at least three years. Schools who have signed up to poor value or non-compliant leases are often not aware of this until the end of the lease term, when it becomes clear what that there is an enormous Residual Value to pay, or that the rules about return of the assets are utterly unreasonable. Ask any lessor that you are seriously considering working with to put you in touch with one of their customer schools that has been through the full lease life cycle. Have a frank conversation, without the lessor present, about whether they'd work with them again.

Ask every company to quote their proposal's 'rate per thousand'. This is a measure of how much it would cost to borrow £1000 pounds from them over a fixed period. It's a 'standard candle' you can use to make like-for-like comparisons. Of course, if they show any resistance to telling you this figure, you already know everything you need to about their ethics.

Ask if the lessor is investing their own money into your deal, if not they are likely brokering in a third party or borrowing the money. This can only mean one thing – two or three companies are making a profit from your lease, which will inevitably be more expensive to you and your parents.

Be extremely cautious of 'all in' solutions that offer to lease you more than just the devices. This is allowable (to a limited extent) but a school should never lease intangibles such as insurance or warranties as this leaves you bearing the risk if the insurance/ warranty provider pulls or varies the policy at any time. You would be tied in to the payments, and possibly left with a product that is not fit for purpose which you cannot cancel. This is a huge risk in the area of insurance, where terms are being tightened constantly at the moment.

The Lease Agreement will contain multiple pages of small-type terms and conditions that attempt to push the financial risk of operating the assets to the lessee – that's you. This is reasonable, in general, as the lessor is seeking to limit their exposure to risks that they cannot otherwise control for. For example, one of the terms will certainly be that the assets are comprehensively insured against loss and damage. Where this becomes less reasonable is through the enforcing of products (e.g. a specific insurer or case type).

Always check the Lease Agreement for "admin" or "document fees". These are stealth fees that can increase the present value of your lease above the approved 89.9% and make it non compliant. They could amount to as much as 10% of the value, which would see the lessor making back all their investment on Day One, and then again at the end when they dispose of the assets!

It is a memorable milestone in your commercial career when you realize that these agreements are not carved in stone but can and should be challenged and amended to better suit the savvy customer:

- Go through the agreement line by line, highlighting all the things that are not clear or which you'd like the lessor to exemplify. Indeed, you may identify clauses which you simply do not accept and would like struck or at least changed. By law, lease agreements have to be written in plain English, but they can still be hard to fully understand so you may want to do this with a colleague.

- Tell the lessor that you'd like to discuss the terms of their proposed agreement and inform them in writing (email is fine) of the clauses you'd like to discuss. This will help them to prepare.

- Meet the lessor and go through your queries and extract from them the commitment to confirm in writing everything that they say to you. Eventually, if you proceed, the Lease Agreement will be changed to reflect what you've agreed.

Examples of unreasonable terms and conditions that you should look out for include:

- A requirement to use a specific supplier of devices or insurance – this will hide a referral fee of some kind. One of the tenets of good commercial practice, remember, is disaggregating packages the industry has put together for your 'convenience';

- Punitive charges which you deem unreasonable for simple administrative changes, for returning devices early, for missing a payment due to error, et cetera;

- Automatic rollover of the lease due to failure to notify the lessor of your intention to terminate. This is a legal requirement of operating leases, but some lessors are more draconian than others in its enforcement. Try to extract reassurances in writing to the effect that you won't automatically trigger a brand new lease just because you send your termination email 89 days before the end date rather than 90.

- Demands to inspect assets at their convenience. This is a hangover from leases designed for business and really isn't practical in school 1-to-1 programmes;

- Unreasonable terms over the return of assets (e.g. that they must be in original packaging, or delivered within a day of the termination date, or fully insured whilst in transit). The ideal outcome here is for the lessor to agree to collect them.

Following this approach tends to elicit one of two responses from lessors – the good companies engage and persevere, the fly-by-nights come up with all sorts of reasons why you're wrong to be asking these questions, before eventually sulking off and refusing to answer emails. It's a little wearying, but ultimately enormously satisfying to be able to quantify precisely how much money you've saved and how many major landmines you've identified and sidestepped. Just think of all the money wasted and risks taken by schools that don't go into this level of diligence...

4.5.2.3 *How to force down the cost of the lease*

The first and most obvious tactic is to talk to several companies rather than just one. We say it's obvious, but with moneylenders, people tend not to shop around for some reason. Create some competition, inject a sense of urgency through a limited window for them to finalize their offer, refuse to travel to them and generally try and set an atmosphere of this being a buyer's rather than a seller's market. This will confuse them, remove the opportunity for traditional sales tactics and hopefully throw into relief those companies who are able to meet your requirements. They're likely to be the ones most motivated to win your business.

It's important to negotiate just as hard with lessors as you would with the supplier of the devices. It is strange that schools seem more comfortable haggling over as little as a pound per device but then accept the first offer made by a money lender, the overall affordability impact of which is far, far greater. It can be hard to do this without breaking the commercial confidences of the other people you are in negotiation with - it is not acceptable to disclose another company's quote, and any lessor who expects you to is sending a message about their own trustworthiness.

The best approach we have found is to keep negotiations non-specific and not to resort to numbers – "You're going to need to do slightly/ quite a bit/ significantly better than that if you're to match the other offers I have on the table" is a useful phrase. Equally, we find that "You are the company that I feel is the best fit for us and you clearly have a lot of integrity, which I really value, but I just can't justify to my Headteacher going with you based on your current prices. It's a real shame... *(pause for effect)*... Well, so long!" works quite effectively too.

Consider a two year rather than three year term. It is cheaper to borrow money for a shorter time, so the overall rental cost is likely to sink from <95% to <90% if you go for a two-year term. Of course, you'll be paying off the same amount borrowed over a shorter time, so it will cost contributors more per month. We've explained this to multiple independent and state schools and the outcome has followed an unwavering pattern; independents that can afford it go for a two-year lease to keep the device as modern as possible whilst reducing the cost of borrowing. State schools almost always go for three to make it more affordable to families. The evaluation after the first year of 1-to-1 carried out with parents of Longfield Academy[33] pointed strongly towards a feeling that what they were asking for (£16 per month over 3 years) did not represent value for money. State schools are investing a good deal of their own money (around 30% on average, in my experience) to bring this cost to parents down as far as possible.

The next tip is about the structure of payment that you will need to agree, which will always be in advance rather than arrears. Annual rental payments tend to be cheaper than quarterly or monthly ones, for the simple reason that you are paying off more money sooner so the balance has less time to attract interest. As long as your school's Business Manager is in agreement with this approach (it's a bigger payment, made in advance of the collection of any contributions, so cash flow may be an issue), you should always opt for Annual rental payments. The cost difference will become obvious if you ask your lessor to quote on all three rental payment cycles.

Ask the lessor to structure the balance of payments more heavily into the Residual Value rather than the Rentals. This is known as loading the back end, rather than the front end of the lease. This pushes more of the burden of paying for the lessor's costs onto whoever buys the devices after you've

---

[33] Clark, M & Luckin, R (2013) 'iPads in the Classroom' London Knowledge Lab, p24.

finished operating them, and most often this will be a third party rather than your parents. The flip side is that the rentals (which, by proxy, your parents do have to pay) are reduced. There's limited scope for flexibility, perhaps a percentage point overall, but it all adds up.

Finally, ask about the possibility of a non-return allowance. This is far from standard but some of the best lessors out there will agree to a small percentage of devices being written off (e.g. not returned), giving you some leeway in the case of devices which are lost, stolen or damaged outside the terms of your insurance. Without this, the terms of the lease will be that 100% of devices are returned in an operational condition, and you'll have to pay the value of those you cannot.

4.5.2.4 Managing a lease going forward

You will need to ensure that you record and track all serial numbers of assets as, in the case of insurance claims leading to replacement devices, you must advise the lessor of any new serial numbers replacing old. This happens when a device is lost/ damaged beyond economic repair and is therefore replaced by the insurer. The lessor's T&Cs will state that you have to tell them (within a certain timeframe) that the old asset has gone and a new, equivalent asset has replaced it. If you don't, they are within their rights to reject this new asset when it comes time to hand it back and enforce the clause that makes you pay for another one.

Equally importantly, ensure that you understand your obligations on serving notice to cancel a lease. As noted about, three months (90 days) is industry standard but some lessors request 12 months. It's not hard to serve notice (though it must be done in writing), but it's also not hard to imagine a school failing to do so, particularly with the churn that goes on with staffing. If a key person (e.g. you!) leaves, how will the institutional memory know what to do? The school's finance department should have a system in place for tracking contracts and their expiry dates – the termination notice date should be added to that. If you have not given notice to cancel/ return/ retain within the correct timeframe your agreement will roll on for an additional rental (which could be a month, a quarter or a year, depending on how you agreed the payment structure).

Similarly, whatever the terms that you agreed over the return of assets at the start of the lease term are, you should plan early how you are going to meet them. It can be very hard to recover assets from pupils if they've chosen not to make the final payment – colleagues of ours have had to resort to knocking on doors and then unravelling the myriad excuses about where the device currently is. It may take several weeks' preparation before you can return all of the assets, which is why it's quite useful to have negotiated a more relaxed attitude from the lessor at the outset.

5 INFRASTRUCTURE & OTHER DEAL-BREAKERS

You will have already heard this many times before from practically everyone you've mentioned this 1-to-1 project to, so we'll spare you the doom-saying and sharp intakes of breath. You know infrastructure is important, but you might not yet appreciate how broad the problem is. This chapter aims to fix that.

No matter how well prepared a school thinks it is (and we've seen this happen in multi-million pound new builds as well as schools that have just spent six figures on cabling, switches and wireless), 1-to-1 will brutally expose every weakness in your technological backbone. It will do it one problem at a time, as just as you think that everything will (finally!) start to flow smoothly, the next bottleneck in the system is ruthlessly revealed.

Why is it virtually impossible to foresee and counteract this? Mostly because it's really hard to simulate what will happen when up to a thousand data-hungry devices are introduced to a network, and their unpredictable owners encouraged to use them all the time and in every place possible. Your technical team's previous experience is of a different world and a different paradigm.

But it's not just what we would traditionally call infrastructure (the largely invisible stuff in the walls) that it is essential to get right, there is also the question of integration with the school's current file system and the none too simple issue of how you make it all work with classroom audio visual equipment.

The need to come up with good answers to all these questions of infrastructure is, alongside the challenge of supporting staff through the change, the main reason why schools implement over a couple of years rather than one. Year one should be about discovering problems, finding solutions and then scaling up. Without this preparation, it seems inevitable that confidence in the project will suffer repeated blows as 'one thing after another' prevents teachers and pupils from making simple, reliable and effective use of these undoubtedly powerful devices.

Plan to avoid that and resist the pressure to just 'get it done'. Get it done right.

Section 5.1 Networks – cables and switches

Behind pretty much every aspect of your school's use of technology sits the dreaded network. You'll have heard it mentioned caustically in early morning briefings when it's 'down', or referred to by bored pupils looking at unresponsive log-in screens when it's 'being slow'. The network is the circulatory system of the school's body, pushing data to where it needs to go, be that a wired PC in your classroom, the digital screen in reception or the Wireless Access Point (WAP) blinking manically on the ceiling.

It goes without saying that unless the network performs well, as it's the starting point for all data-enabled activities, everything will work poorly, no matter how new, shiny and aspirational the packaging. To paraphrase Michael Gove, no school's use of technology can exceed the quality of its network. (Admittedly the key words we've changed there are 'education system' and 'teachers').

The main issue with school networks is one of historic underinvestment. What your 1-to-1 project calls for is a managed network built from high-capacity fibre optic and modern copper cabling, held together by switches capable of massive throughput and intelligent traffic routing, all ideally made by a single manufacturer. This is probably £100k or so of kit, none of it more than two to three years old.

What you almost certainly have at the moment, if you are like the average school, is a system that's been pieced together over several years using whatever was available at the time, with the limited funding that Heads tend to grant for stuff that they can't see and which never seems to make much of a difference anyway.

School Network Managers, to be fair, have had it pretty tough – they're held to account against infrastructures that they probably didn't design (and may never have even been designed) and which have grown organically and in an ad hoc manner, slowly spidering out from the centre to create a sprawling hinterland of switches and cables. Each new post holder will have layered their organisational and product preferences onto a system that no one probably fully understands and isn't documented or labelled. To sum up, school networks are usually a bit of a mess.

Here are the key questions to ask about your network infrastructure;

- Is the data cabling and set up in the core (linking together the stacks of switches in the server room) and edge (in switch rooms, or more likely wall-hung cabinets) capable of delivering a throughput of 10Gbps (Gigabits per second)? Every byte of data must flow through this channel, so it needs to be wide enough to cope. The cables concerned should be modern (less than 5 years old) fibre optic, with 24 cores to provide scalable growth.

- Do the core switches in the server room have the capacity to handle the throughput of data that the multitude of cables will be delivering to them? At least 10Gbps will be required.

- Are the cables running between the core and the edge switch room cabinets of similar specification to those mentioned in the first bullet point above? This is the next potential drag factor on performance, when the network is segmented and data starts to move out to the various blocks/ wings/ buildings of the school.

- Are the switches at edge that will serve your Wireless Access Points manageable, Layer 3 and capable of delivering Power over Ethernet (PoE)? Be aware of 50v and 24v standards, as some WAPs need more power. Most managed Wireless Access Points benefit greatly from this technology as it eliminates the scenario whereby the cleaner disconnects the access point's power to plug in their vacuum cleaner. Modern access points are capable of transmissions over 100mbps, therefore a compatibility with gigabit PoE standards is desirable.

- Ideally, you'd want every switch in the school to be from the same Tier 1 manufacturer (e.g. Cisco or HP – a good rule of thumb being if you recognise the brand from a supermarket, it's probably not what your school needs). A single manufacturer makes it so much easier to manage the switches in a common interface, to troubleshoot problems, to monitor performance and also reduces the risk of incompatibility. Many of the older type of switches won't be manageable, meaning that you can't tweak how they are set up or even see how they are performing.

- Is the copper network cabling running from edge switches to the Wireless Access Points at least Category 5e? Cat5e is a specification (now superseded by Cat6 generally) that can carry enough data to ensure a 1Gbps flow to the WAP.

- Are the core switches capable of supporting multicast routing to simplify the handling of traffic related over-the-air services that tablets often use? In the Apple world this relies on a service called Bonjour being allowed to pass through the various layers of security that wireless systems use to block traffic they don't recognise. The Bonjour service enables AirPlay (screen mirroring) and AirPrint (which does what you think it does), among other things. Systems that are unable, or require very complex re-plumbing, to allow this type of data to flow smoothly are the cause of more angst among teachers and technical teams that anything else in nascent 1-to-1 schools, because so much of the value of tablet devices relies on being to instantly share what you are doing via a large screen.

- Is the Network IP schema setup to allow for a thousand additional devices to operate on your network? Do you VLAN them off your main production network for security or just have a large flat VLAN where everything is permitted to talk to everything? A class C network with 250 odd available addresses is unlikely to cut the mustard.

It is essential that you find out the answers to these 'minimum' spec questions before planning a timeline for 1-to-1 deployment, as the resolution of any major problems found, particularly if cabling is involved, will be expensive and will probably have to wait for a summer holiday. As mentioned in the introduction to this chapter, plan to spend Year 1 addressing your infrastructure.

Without wanting to do anyone a disservice, it is not unknown for school Network Managers to refute some of the specifications set out above, claiming that they are over the top. This is an understandable reaction to the intrusion into their expert domain of a user with a little bit of knowledge. With respect, if they haven't experienced the full shock of a one device per user school, they are almost certainly underestimating the scale of problem. It is worth referring here to Section 3.1.3 about the necessity of 'on message technical staff'.

A good solution is to commission a survey by a cabling and networking company with whom the school has an existing relationship. Ensure they are fully briefed as to your ambitions and the quantity and type of devices you are talking about. Such surveys are usually free of charge, as they are a necessary precursor to the work being carried out. Even if chargeable (maybe up to a couple of thousand pounds), it will be money well spent in the medium term.

Section 5.2 Wireless

Wireless networks were a revelation when they started to be widely implemented at the turn of the century. They've now come to play such a huge role in the life of most schools, it is difficult to imaging coping without access to data over the air, wherever it is needed.

Unfortunately, wireless networking is inherently more problematic than its dull, agoraphobic but usually pretty reliable wired older brother. It works by transmitting data using specific frequencies of the radio spectrum and, because pretty much everything else does this too these days and the spectrum is quite a crowded place, it can be subject to interference.

Wireless can also be pretty ineffective at penetrating solid objects such as walls. Even the number of people in a room can affect how far the signal travels, as we block and absorb radio wave energy just as effectively as any other dense collection of carbon, hydrogen and oxygen atoms. To make matters worse, if your school was built in the last fifteen years, it's probably something of a Faraday cage, seeing as modern architects are obsessed with highly reflective glass and builders love a steel frame clad with concrete.

An important concept to grasp is that wireless in a large, distributed network is very different from that which you probably have at home. As soon as you introduce any complexity (e.g. a second Wireless Access Point), you need to configure how the WAPs are prevented from interfering with each other, whilst still delivering the same transparent service to users. Add in another 100 of them, and your Network Manager will need a PhD in Euclidian geometry just to face coming to work every morning.

This is why modern Enterprise-level wireless systems are intelligently self-managing and, at a simplistic level, learn the layout of your building, monitor what's going on with data and make constant, tiny adjustments to:

- ensure that connections aren't dropped as users move around your building;
- balance data loads between available WAPs where high concentrations of devices are found;

- adjust WAPs' broadcast strength to avoid overlapping and generally work to keep the whole thing from grinding to a halt.

You may have experienced wireless where the signal is weak in certain rooms, where the connection drops out if you move, where speed slows to a crawl when more than a few devices are connected, where you can connect but can't get the Internet to work, where you can see a distant, weak access point but can't get your computer to recognize the one you're stood under... the list of problems you've experienced yourself possibly continues. The most likely cause is the same as the problems with school wired networks described above – seldom have schools had sufficient resources, or maybe the need, to put appropriately robust and featured wireless networks in place.

Another big change that your 1-to-1 project will bring is the type of things that your school's wireless will be called upon to deliver. Teachers and students will be constantly and concurrently accessing streaming video from the Internet, creating a lot of traffic. They will also be pushing their devices' screens wirelessly to classroom projectors using complex, proprietary and frankly highly-strung protocols such as Airplay. You will want different layers of security to apply to different types of users and for access to the wireless network to be linked to their usernames and passwords rather than knowledge of a secret key. The appropriateness of your wireless network will not only be judged by how much data it can handle – of far greater importance will be how well it can cope with these new types of usage. It is this misconception (that speed is all that matters) that most often trips up schools who think their existing systems are good enough.

Here are the key questions to ask about your wireless network;

- Does it support the modern range of wireless 'standards', technically known as 802.11a/b/g or n? Older systems tend only to support devices in the a/b/g standards, which are less powerful and slower. Most current tablets/ laptops will support at least n.

- Can the system support multiple different SSIDs? These are the differently named networks that you see in large buildings, usually called things like 'Guest' or 'Conference 1' et cetera. These are actually logically separated wireless networks pushed out by a single system. You will want the ability to provide different levels of access to different users – for example, you might want users of the 'Staff' SSID to have access to screen mirroring, or for users of 'Guest' to only have access to three specifically white-listed websites.

- Does the system support 802.11x authentication, often referred to as 'Radius'? This allows users to connect to wireless networks using their standard network username and password. This is much more secure (only users who have a school identity can connect to certain networks). Without this, you will have to rely on a centrally-set wireless password to prevent pupil access to the staff wireless network. As this password can be fairly easily gleaned in various ways, it will usually be back in circulation amongst students before break-time, necessitating every teacher having to re-enter the new password… Repeat ad infinitum.

- Does it have a feature (usually called a 'gateway') to simplify the handling of traffic related to the over-the-air services that tablets use? See the section above for why this is so critical to printing and screen sharing.

- Is it able to self-manage the estate of WAPs to ensure that coverage responds to demand in localized areas and adjusts itself to suit users as they move around?

- Are there sufficient WAPs (or cabling for them) in teaching spaces? Current best practice is to have a WAP per classroom minimum, and a redundant data point to support a second (which should be located towards the opposite side of the room).

- Do your large spaces, where pupils are likely to spend free/ social time and where large groups may be taught, feature sufficient depth of coverage? For example, in school halls you might see 4-8 WAPs, typically. Examination procedures will inevitably enter the 21st

Century at some point soon – it's wise to plan for enough data per English GCSE candidate sat in the gym.

- Has consideration been given to outside areas and how to serve them with wireless coverage? They are, after all, heavily used social and learning spaces and not just by the PE department. It is usually possible to provide targeted cones of coverage via WAPs mounted on the external walls of buildings. If a particularly remote yet critical area needs wireless, you may need to run power and data cabling out to a suitable position to mount a WAP.

Similarly to the wired network, the simplest way of getting a neutral assessment of the above issues is through a wireless survey from a potential provider. This can be especially useful in establishing how much investment is needed, particularly as the density of WAPs needed may surprise you.

Section 5.3 Bandwidth & filtering

5.3.1.   Bandwidth

We're old enough to remember when our schools first got broadband. We're also not so proud that we can't admit that we didn't really know what it was. It was a pre-wireless era of half-sets (half-sets!) of PCs around the fringes of a few classrooms. The first school broadband was 2Mbps and it felt like lightning. Ah, salad days!

Funnily enough, the pathetic 2Mbps we often get at home is now the speed at which our Netflix starts to stutter and we find we can't send emails at the same time. We have all become unknowing and gradual victims of bandwidth inflation as the services we use have multiplied, bloated and become somewhat vampiric (just think of all those apps on your smartphone or tablet that sit on your home wireless sucking down new data every 30 seconds). Don't even get us started on the implications of the next wave of smart fridges, fire alarms and Internet-enabled loo seats.

It is the same in our schools. 2Mbps became 10, 10 became 50 and now, we are reliably informed by an industry association that the majority of secondary schools have or plan within a year to have a 100Mbps connection. Sounds like a lot, eh?

The inflationary effect here is more caused by the number of devices schools now have, coupled with wireless networks that connect them to the Internet from anywhere. Your school will probably have hundreds of tablets, laptops and maybe even a few forlorn PCs sharing your bandwidth at any time. This sharing is known in technical circles as the 'contention ratio' and the sum isn't hard to do;

Total bandwidth divided by number of concurrent devices.

Thus even a 100Mbps connection is experienced by the 50th concurrent user as, effectively, 2Mbps. It's not quite as simple as we're making out, because it depends what those users are doing at the time, but you get the general idea.

So, fast forward by a year or two and do the same sum. In our 'average' secondary school with 1000 pupils and 100 teachers, it's probable that around 275 devices will be in active use at any one time (but bear in mind that they will all be passively grazing data in the background). A 100Mbps connection at that level of contention will deliver an experience equivalent to about a third of a Megabyte per second – 0.36Mbps. That wouldn't have been enough to update your MySpace page or Ask Jeeves even the simplest of questions back in 2004, so forget about uploading that iMovie of your science experiment to the departmental YouTube channel.

It really is time to turn the dial up to 11.

Here are the key considerations for bandwidth;

- Find out the current speed of the connection and what your usage graphs look like. You'll know if your bandwidth is already insufficient because it will be regularly getting in the way of lessons and admin. Your Network Manager will be able to get stats from your provider showing when traffic peaks and if it maxes-out your allowance. You may be able to use this, combined with a knowledge of how many mobile devices you currently have to work out a very rough approximation of what you might need in the future.

- However, it's an accepted norm to double whatever number that exercise spits out, a little like your GP does when they ask about your alcohol consumption. In a successful 1-to-1 school, pupils will have constant personal access to a device (not occasional access to the institution's). Their entire learning life will be tied into these devices, which will also be constantly popping online all on their own to get email, check for updates, and refresh the data behind a hundred apps. You will probably also have moved your storage into the cloud. It's an entirely different beast and in the immortal words of Roy Schneider, "You're gonna need a bigger boat".

- If you currently have a reasonably fast connection, you shouldn't need to put in place a new 'circuit' – this is what BT call the fibre going from the roadside cabinet into your server room. As you can guess, with all the ground works required, this can run to tens of thousands and take several months. Getting a quote to upgrade your connection will reveal whether this is the case.

- However, even on an existing circuit, putting in place an upgraded connection can still be incredibly long-winded and frustrating, with lead times of 90 days being standard and the quality of communication from the various parties involved routinely atrocious. This is one change you'll certainly want to schedule over a summer holiday. In fact, here's an even better idea: schedule it for late June so that when the work is eventually done (a month or so late), it falls neatly into the quiet period of early August.

- The minimum recommended Internet bandwidth for a 1-to-1 secondary school would be 100Mbps. We know of many who have gone to 200Mbps and one which now has 300Mbps.

- Future scalability is also an important consideration when buying a new connection. The commonly used metaphor is that of pipework. Connections are described as being X over a Y 'bearer', with X being the speed of water flow and Y the capacity of the pipe. Thus 200Mbps over a 1000Mbps (a 'Gig', more accurately) bearer, leaves a lot of headroom should you want, for example, to turn the tap up a little bit next year to 300 or even 400Mbps as the scale of demand becomes clearer. Likewise, you can scale it back, particularly in August, to reduce your rental slightly. It's cheaper to buy narrower 'pipes' regardless of the 'flow', but it's short-sighted.

- If you do need to upgrade your connection, there is some good news – it's never been cheaper or more competitive. Gone are the days when only Regional Broadband Consortia could offer schools affordable connections, and a 100Mbps over a 1000Mbps bearer now only costs around £6,000 per year. The market varies hugely around the country, so you'll need to do your own investigations.

- One additional and highly sensible provision which can make your bandwidth stretch a great deal further is the use of a caching server. The job of this device is to pre-emptively download all the app and OS updates to one central location and then distribute them out to pupils' tablets as they connect to the local network. This avoids 1000 pupils arriving at school on a Monday morning and triggering 1000 separate downloads of a 1Gb update. This is particularly vital when considering that major OS updates can be 2-8Gb in size, and that they always seem to happen in the first week of September.

5.3.2   Filtering

If you are moving your connectivity, it's a good time to reconsider your filtering. Indeed, you may need to pick a new filtering solution if this was previously done upstream by your Internet Service Provider or RBC. Local provision is always preferable to having someone else control your filtering, so this should be seen as a positive step by teachers and technical staff alike.

Parental concerns about their children being exposed to inappropriate content are adequately addressed by in-school filters, which ensure that the websites that pupils have access to whilst on-site are appropriate. Some filtering products go a step further though and allow all Internet traffic going through a device, regardless of the network it is connected to, to be passed through the school's filters. What this means in practical terms is that when they're using the Internet on their device at home, the school's strict filtering policies will still apply.

A concern that often emerges is that children can connect their school-issued device via Bluetooth to their mobile phone in their pocket, using the phone's 3 or 4G connection as a private, unfiltered Internet connection that is entirely beyond the school's control. This is really hard to spot without frequently scanning for mobile hotspots, as the use of the tablet appears legitimate - it's the secreted hotspot (the phone in the pocket) that is the illicit behaviour.

Assuming that you don't want to technically block all mobile signals in the school (which is expensive and impractical), this method of gaining unfiltered access to the Internet is best dealt with as a behaviour management problem. Include the use of hotspots as prohibited activity in your AUP, and enforce this by periodically scanning for active hotspots in different parts of the school and applying sanctions to offenders. You won't catch every instance, but you only really need to make a high-profile example out of a few unfortunates to ensure it stays a niche activity.

A further thing to factor in is that some MDM companies (see Section 5.7) also produce web filters and their two products fit very neatly into a single solution.

You can expect to pay £2k-8k per annum for a filtering solution, depending on the product, the features selected and the amount of traffic you need to filter. The lower end of this scale is probably sufficient.

Section 5.4 Joined-up systems

One of many problems which beset early-adopters of 1-to-1 in schools was the entirely separate nature of the systems they were introducing (and generally we are talking about iPads here) and those that the school had been using for years (and here we're talking Microsoft networks and Office software).

Staff and pupils at your school almost certainly will have the same issue – all their work is currently stored in their network user area, all their collaborative documents are in a shared drive, and everything is in .doc, .ppt, .xls, and .pub format. The introduction of a new device which does not allow users to log into the school's Microsoft network and seems to store all its files in a separate little box per app can be confusing, silo-ed and makes some question the usefulness of introducing such a 'disconnected' device.

Parents have strong views on this too, we have found. Many see great value in their child understanding Microsoft Office packages and knowing how Windows works, and with some justification as it is likely to remain the cornerstone of many businesses' use of technology for some time.

Of course, these arguments skate over the other benefits of devices like the iPad (the collaboration, creativity, independence, et cetera) and the fact that very often schools choose them precisely because they are *not* capable of running PowerPoint, but let's leave that to one side for now and concentrate on the criticisms and problems that you will have to deal with.

The crux of the issue is that school networks are designed to be secure and to only allow specific devices running specific software to access them; there is no simple way to connect an iPad to a Windows network. This means that students can't get to their work that's stored on the network and equally can't get their iPad work off the tablet and onto the school network. It's not fun trying to work from two places at once. Try it – the thing you really need is always in the other place and maintaining two separate file systems is a real pain. Eventually you stop doing it.

There are horrible, labour-intensive workarounds (like emailing everything to yourself, or using insecure cloud storage like Dropbox as an online USB stick) but that way lies madness. You have been fairly warned.

No, if any 1-to-1 project is to be a success, it has to remove barriers for students rather than create new ones, it needs to integrate with existing structures and use them to add value. If it can, along the way, win the hearts and minds of the most die-hard Microsoft users, all the better (and by the way, if you solve the integration concern, it usually does). To scale new heights of ridiculous hyperbole and risk probable heresy, it reminds us of the bit in the New Testament where Jesus says: "Think not that I am come to destroy the Law or the Prophets. I am not come to destroy, but to fulfil". Yes, it's exactly like that.

Moving on. Happily, in March of 2014, Office for iPad was finally allowed to slope its way out of the Microsoft stable, a day late and a dollar short, but at least it was available. iPad users could now view MS Office documents on their tablet to their heart's content (they just couldn't edit them, for which you need an Office 365 subscription, see below). This goes some way to placating those who see Office as an essential workplace skill.

The key to success here is finding a way to allow iPads (and other non-Microsoft tablets) to access user data on the school's network, in as frictionless a manner as possible. There are two types of solution:

5.4.1   Middleware

Tools that are based on a technology called WebDav, such as Securlink and Foldr are effective, but have a cost:

- They work by installing a piece of server software on the school's network and an app on the tablet;

- Functionally, the user logs into the app using their school network username and password, and then they can see their user area and any shared drives they have the rights to, and can move files between the tablet and these folders;

- The frequency with which users have to authenticate in this way can be adjusted;

- What's happening in the background is that the server-side part of the application is communicating with the network's Active Directory service to pass through the credentials sent from the tablet app;

- It doesn't work in reverse (e.g. you can't log onto a PC to dig files out of the tablet, you already need to have moved them onto the network from the tablet to be able to see them in Windows);

- It's not quite as intuitive as saving a file locally, which you would expect; there are three or four steps to the process;

- The bottom line is that it works and, at a stroke, the two systems are to all intents and purposes joined. Expect to pay £2-4k per annum for services such as these.

5.4.2   Cloud storage

This is unquestionably the better solution, based on both cost and functionality, but represents a significant project in its own right:

- The way this works is by turning the problem on its head – you move all your user data (everyone's files and all shared areas) into the cloud. Obviously this needs to be secure and manageable, but both methods described below tick those boxes. The benefit is that you can now get to your files from anywhere that you can get an Internet connection and the whole issue of trying to poke a secure hole in the school's network dissolves in a puff of, well 'precipitating water vapour' would be the appropriate metaphor;

- An additional and enormous benefit is one of cost and effort. Once you move away from hosting all your data in your server room, you don't need to buy any more storage or pay to maintain it. See Section 4.2.3 above for more detail on this;

- Both Microsoft and Google offer free-to-education cloud storage as part of their Office 365 and Apps for Education (GAFE) services, respectively;

- Both offer vast amounts of free storage on their cloud drives (Microsoft's OneDrive is a whopping 1 Terabyte per user at the time of writing. That ought to be enough for the duration of anyone's schooling. Google have gone a step further - there is no limit on file storage for GAFE users). We can't see this being diminished as the cost of storage continues to decline and the cloud-storage market gets ever more aggressively competitive;

- Both allow you to log in using your school network credentials (username and password). With Microsoft's service, this is a requirement, with Google there is a free add-on tool that syncs users' Microsoft credentials with their Google identities;

- Both are 'free' but there is an underlying cost. With Microsoft, O365 (Plan A2 to be precise) is free to schools that already license their products under the Enrolment for Education Services agreement (EES). You probably already have this as it's the most cost-effective way of licensing Windows and Office for schools. For Google, the cost is one of change – you need to move your email and calendaring over to the Google platform really to make the environment function effectively. There are ways of forwarding Exchange-based email to Gmail, but we've not found them very satisfactory;

- To enable O365, there's a migration process to follow, that can be quite involved and technically challenging. Many schools have sought (and received) help from Microsoft to achieve this. Again, it moves not just your storage but your email and calendaring off-premises too.

Our recommendation to schools that already have an EES and make any use of Office is to follow the Microsoft O365 route, partly because it is simpler than the GAFE and has more continuity of skills for users, partly because it's better integrated into Office and mostly because of something called **Student Advantage**. Under this scheme, once a school has created O365 accounts for its pupils, they are entitled to download 5 free licences for Office, to deploy anywhere. This is really very valuable – they can install it on their mum's laptop, Granddad's PC, anywhere they might occasionally need it for school work. Most critically, though, it unlocks the Office for iPad apps and allows pupils to edit as well as view files. One slight caveat to this is that staff have to pay (roughly £17 per annum currently) to unlock the mobile apps, although this is shortly to become free.

One final consideration, however, is your workflow solution, which you really need to tie in with all of these decisions as it's the bit of your 1-to-1 solution that will affect every user, every lesson. Please see the advice on this in Chapter 6. If you are going down the Google Classroom route, then a GAFE domain with Google-powered email and storage makes more sense.

Section 5.5 Printing

If this section feels counter intuitive to you, you're in good company. A truly successful 1-to-1, with well-embedded workflows and a genuine culture of digital outputs does not need to worry itself with printing. Everything whizzes through the ether, from pupil to teacher and back again in the blink of an idealised eye. Indeed, you possibly sold the idea to your employers partly on the promise of reducing your paper bill to zero. If something is needed in paper format, coursework maybe, it could always be printed from a PC (as long as you've joined up your systems - see Section 5.4), but fundamentally you will have moved your institution into the post-print age.

There are, in actuality, two paths here. The first is as described above - a scorched earth, none-shall-pass approach which removes the ability and, over time, the desire to print stuff out the whole time. The 'no printing' thing is quite hard to achieve and will make you about as popular with your colleagues as a failed Ofsted inspector who has decided to turn their hand to cold-calling at tea time to sell pet insurance.

The second path is a compromise of everything that is pure and true about the shift to 1-to-1, but might just be what you need to do to help staff transition to new ways of working. There are fairly simple ways of making printers talk to tablets wirelessly, although you will need printers that are compatible with whichever protocol your devices use. It's not the gleaming new dawn you dreamed of, but that's education for you.

All joking aside, the risk of this compromised approach does need careful consideration. It is for you to decide if it provides transitional support through a major change, or whether it actually undermines the things you're trying to achieve, allowing people to stick to tasks that lead to printing (research and presentation, typically) rather than attempting the new types of learning activity that this technology for the first time makes possible. Some schools that have enabled printing have actually seen their print volumes increase, which is logical as every child now has the ability to make stuff and send it to the printer, every lesson. It's also worth thinking about the extra data traffic created by services like AirPrint - turning this off can help resolve networking issues.

Section 5.6 Audio Visual integration

If you've been reading this book sequentially rather than dipping in as needed, you're probably a little tired of hearing that this or that particular aspect of 1-to-1 is *the* most important and *the* single thing you can't afford to get wrong. Well, this time we really, *really* mean it.

It's hard to explain what it feels like the first time you see a lesson in a 1-to-1 environment that makes use of really effective screen mirroring by both staff and students. Something indefinable but almost tangible changes about the classroom dynamic. It may be that the teacher no longer feels the need to stand at the front, tethered to the whiteboard, but spends the lesson working alongside the pupils from various tables. It could be that anyone can lead the learning from their seat. It might be that pupils feel that the balance of power has slid perceptibly towards them and that they are now full partners in the lesson, rather than merely present in it. Perhaps it's a combination of these things, whatever – the result is powerful, participative, eager learning and it's a pretty special thing to see.

This atmosphere is achieved by providing staff and students with an instant, simple and reliable way to push their device's screen to the classroom's large display and thereby share whatever they are doing. For the teacher, they suddenly have a handheld visualizer capable of instantly displaying demonstrations of how something is done as well as showing pupils' paper-based work. Students can mirror their screen by invitation to talk through their decisions or seek advice on next steps, which leads to very effective feedback loops of peer- and self-assessment.

It makes us think about the start of our teaching careers, when we'd rush around at break-time getting children's work photocopied onto acetate to display via the creaky and dim OHP. We'd analyse and improve them using a permanent marker and the effect was the same – great investment by the class in an authentic, meaningful piece of learning. Due to the limitations of the technology available, it was rarely possible to do this in a short timeframe, however, which is a vital feature of effective feedback. It also wasn't possible for everyone to see, or to be able to make decisions on the fly within a lesson when a particular opportunity arose. Screen mirroring removes these limitations entirely and optimises the effectiveness of iterative assessment, one of the most well-proven and impactful educational strategies (see the chapter on evidence above).

5.6.1   How is this screen mirroring achieved?

There are different wireless protocols for the different device Operating Systems, but they all do the same thing, which is to allow the video and audio signal from a device to be wirelessly transmitted to something that's connected to the classroom projector or screen. For Apple, this is called Airplay, Windows uses Miracast (pronounced Mirror-cast, we assume) and Android has Chromecast. There is some overlap here, and other less well-known solutions, but let's stick to the well trodden path, as getting mainstream technologies to work well can still be a challenge. Even the best mirroring solution is at the mercy of the room's wireless peculiarities and the occasional drop-out is inevitable. Please see the section on wireless above for advice on this.

You need to have a device connected to the projector or screen by a physical cable. This device decodes the signal being sent by the mobile device whose screen is being mirrored. There are specific hardware products to carry out this role (Apple TV and the Chromecast dongle, most popularly) or you can use a PC or laptop that is running a compatible piece of streaming software (Airserver and Reflector are two examples).

This technology was originally designed for your living room, to let you stream content from your phone or tablet straight to your TV. However, both the hardware and the software products have matured significantly over the last year and are now quite well adapted to the classroom. They include security features that let you display a one-off code so that pupils can share their screens without the teacher worrying about people outside the room being able to hijack the display, as used to be the case when simple passwords were used. It should be noted however that Chromecast, a relatively new product, is not yet at this stage of maturity.

5.6.2   Hardware device or software streamer?

Whichever route you determine is right for your environment, ensure that top of the list of your considerations is this: screen sharing has to work first time, every time, for even the least confident, most resistant and skeptical of colleagues. If the process is unreliable, too technically complex or insecure, it won't be used and your school will be missing out on one of the most powerful educational affordances of 1-to-1 mobile devices.

Hardware solutions are costly, but more reliable than software streamers. The first cost is the unit itself, which in effect is a mini-computer designed to do just this one job. The second, and larger cost is that of physical integration. Apple TV and Chromecast both use an HDMI cable to connect to the display; this is because they're designed for modern TVs, which have multiple HDMI ports as standard. The bad news is that your classroom projector, unless it's relatively new, will not. There are two solutions – replace the projector (the ideal, but least affordable answer) or use a conversion cable (HDMI to VGA). This latter option is cheap but nasty; the cable will have to be from some third party manufacturer and won't carry sound. The final cost is infrastructural; Apple TV and Chromecast need a power socket nearby. This should be up high, where the projector/ screen is. The alternative is a long HDMI cable, with the Apple TV plugged in lower down - but be aware that these devices are prone to disappear if easily accessible. Chromecast can be powered via a USB cable, but it performs better when it is powered off the mains. Only you can judge how expensive this whole piece will be for your school, but in a classroom with all the problems above, to do this right is going to cost around £1000.

A slightly different approach to software streaming is taken by the Microsoft mirroring protocol Miracast. Miracast is an emerging technology and un-reliant on infrastructure, using an ad hoc connection to a Windows PC or laptop. It is a standard allowing open adoption by manufacturers and can be used with Windows 8 and more recent versions Android. The user will connect their mobile device to a device capable of handling Miracasts - in effect your tablet will talk wirelessly to your laptop, if the latter is modern enough. For this reason it is important that is it operated in close proximity within the room. Miracast is 'dumb' and solely dependent of media content being processed by the connected mobile device, so if you put your mobile device to sleep, Miracast will stop.

Using a piece of PC-installed software to stream your screen is attractive for lots of reasons. Firstly it obviates the need to upgrade your displays to be HDMI capable; you can simply connect a PC or laptop via the blue VGA cable as you probably already do. Your sound will continue to function via the PC as it currently does and teachers can quite easily switch between the tablet's image and use of the interactive whiteboard. Secondly, a licence for

Airserver costs about $5, compared to AppleTV's £60+ and Chromecast's £30. That's a big saving when scaled across 100 rooms or more. There are no additional power sockets needed, further simplifying things.

Finally, because this streaming software is partially aimed at the education market, there's a good chance that it will continue to develop classroom-enhancing features. Airserver, for example, already allows you to mirror two screens side by side, and to record what you are mirroring.

There is also a growing range of classroom-focused mirroring software designed to bridge the gap between IWB and tablet - Samsung's Smart School, Promethean's Classflow and Displaynote all allow content to be pushed from the teacher to the student's device. It's mirroring in reverse, if you like.

Steady on though, because all is not rosy in the software streaming garden. What Apple TV and Chromecast do so effectively is remove hardware variables from the streaming equation, ensuring that the wireless protocol works really well, on a known, optimised hardware configuration. Expecting your classroom PC (which is usually a fairly low-spec and aging machine) or laptop (rarely featuring a powerful enough video card) to do the job equally well would likely prove to be a mistake. There are also more things to go wrong and fox the 'average' teacher, making them less likely to persist with screen mirroring. The best approach, as ever, is to try things out on a small scale before making any big decisions.

5.6.3   The 'ideal' trial classroom AV setup

It's hard to be definitive as things vary so much from school to school, but all things being equal, if we were trialling how best to set up a classroom for use with 1-to-1 devices, We'd do the following:

1.   Convince your head to give you a budget for this investigation – it will be money well spent if you can avoid implementing a flawed model that will plague every teacher in every lesson.

2. Find a willing teacher to act as a guinea pig. They need to be a strong practitioner, relatively tech-savvy, with a positive 'can do' attitude to new things and who won't be phased by the occasional failure. Ideally, this teacher would be you, as you need to fully understand the pros and cons of each solution you trial, but that may not be practical.

3. Pick the classroom that your guinea pig does most of their teaching in to use for your testing. Bear in mind that anyone else timetabled into this space may have problems using your set-up.

4. Rip out all the old AV – whiteboard, projector, speakers, fixed PC or laptop connection box – and start from scratch with a nice, clean, painted wall featuring a double power socket directly behind where the screen will go.

5. Talk to a decent educational AV company to identify a non-interactive flat display panel, the kind made for commercial rather than domestic use (as it will be more robust and have fewer things pupils can fiddle with). For a standard classroom, it needs to measure at least 70" diagonally. This is smaller than most whiteboards, but because the image is backlit and much clearer, it's a viable size. It should have built-in speakers and at least two HDMI ports. The cost of this will be between £1500 and £2000, though the right supplier might be excited enough about what you're doing to be convinced to work in partnership with you.

6. Buy the streaming box that best suits your OS and plug it in.

7. Equip your guinea pig teacher with the device you are actively considering loaded with several different whiteboarding applications (see Section 8.2.2), and a £25 voucher for the OS's app store, so that they can try out new things.

8. Abandon current practices. Forget about your whiteboard flipcharts and PowerPoint resources and try and live in 1-to-1

world as fully as possible. This is controversial and challenging, which is why you are trialling rather than implementing en masse.

9. Set up a schedule of evaluations and lesson observations to capture what is discovered about the appropriateness of this solution, and meet to research and plan solutions to the problems found.

5.6.4.1 *Why are we recommending this set up?*

Mostly because it makes a break with practices and safety-nets which might otherwise become stultifying to give staff more opportunities to passively resist. You will note that there is no PC in this set up. Many lessons will otherwise continue to focus on content transmission, gatekept by the adult with control of the whiteboard pens. No one wants to think this of one's colleagues, but this is a genuine barrier to progress that each 1-to-1 school will have to overcome somehow. Hardwiring a solution into your AV set up is a bold but unsubvertable answer.

The hardware selected is the most reliable and simple solution for screen mirroring. There's very little to go wrong.

An LED panel, rather than a projector, is a good economic choice in the medium term, as it will continue to produce a great image for 50,000 hours without needing expensive bulb replacements. It will also not suffer the colour fading and washing out we see so often with Interactive Whiteboards (IWBs). A slightly cheaper solution, though with a much less bright and clear image, can be achieved with a lampless projector such as those made by Casio.

The lack of 'front of class' interactivity (the screen is dumb) forces the effective use of the device to interact with the display. This is inherently more flexible and democratic. Don't waste money on expensive interactive flat panels – they cost twice what a dumb panel does and echo Interactive Whiteboard practices of yesteryear. However, Interactive Flat Panel

Displays (IFPDs) may be a good transitional step away from IWBs, if you are nervous about the pace of change we are suggesting.

Section 5.7 Device Management

This isn't the most exciting Section of the book, let's get that on the table from the start. But it is quite an important one, so please don't skip past Device Management thinking that this is aimed at technical types - anyone running a 1-to-1 project needs to understand the principles too. This is because poor device management controls are a threat to the success of your project. Every time a pupil disrupts a lesson on the other side of the school by posting something inflammatory to a social network, or every time a parent complains that their child is misusing the device at home and their behaviour has changed, you will need to rely on your device management solution to resolve the issues. Also, without a tool which eases the deployment of large numbers of devices, set-up is a burden and on-going management is down to the skill and interest of the individual user. And we all know how that will pan out.

The history of device management is nasty, brutish and short, but happily you've timed your arrival well and have missed all the really terrible bits. As mobile devices became mainstream, schools were keen to explore the impact they could have on learning. Unfortunately, a growing consumer market didn't cater for large scale education deployments and a system of workarounds and guesswork ensued. Fortunately, device management has caught up with the device adoption rate in the form of Mobile Device Management (MDM) systems. Consequently individuals can control and manage a 1-to-1 device environment from a central location without the need to physically handle each device. This approach is strongly recommended for large scale deployments.

MDM solutions allow an administrator to enrol devices, configure and update settings, install apps and set restrictions all within a secure environment. This means a new device can be configured for a student to meet the requirements for learning with little setup time. Often a student will only be required to enter login details and check that the configuration is correct with the support of IT staff. Post-setup this also means the device can be managed remotely, via the wireless network, allowing the administrator to push updates or control restrictions as appropriate.

Let's take two typical 1-to-1 school scenarios to illustrate the impact an MDM solution can have.

5.7.1   Chromebook/ Chrome tablet Management

Chromebooks/ Chrome tablets are managed through the Chrome browser using their 'Chrome device management' tool. At the time of writing, this licence costs £19 per device. The tool allows the administrator to configure Chrome's features for the students (by setting rights based on their Google Apps for Education login), set up access to Wi-Fi networks and pre-install Chrome apps and extensions on the device. The options available to each student are personal even though the settings may be set by the institution. Granular control levels extend to the creation of 'organisational units'. This means the administrator can apply settings to the whole school, year groups, class sets or individuals as appropriate.

The management tool is located on the web-based Admin Console that the administrator can access behind their domain login. The Chrome settings are separated into five sections for ease of use:

- User settings - These can be set by the administrator or set to allow the student to choose certain settings. Control ranges from the ability to block apps and extensions to the specification of a home page for all. This is also where the administrator can publish private Chrome web apps or purchase app packs for education in bulk.
- Public session settings - This allows multiple users to share the same device without requiring a user to sign in with their Google login. Useful for shared carts of devices.
- Device settings - This allows a specific device to be configured for school use and maintains those settings regardless of a student logging in using a school or public Google login.

- Network settings - Configures Wi-Fi settings for all Chrome devices enrolled within the school domain. VPN settings can also be configured here.
- Chrome devices - Allows the administrator to view all Chrome device details centrally.

5.7.2   MacBook/ iPad Management

Just like Chromebooks, the operating systems for Apple Mac and iPads, OS X and iOS, have built in MDM software that allows third party MDM solutions to wirelessly interact with Apple devices. A range of Apple products can all be configured and managed from a central location in school. Features supported by the MDM solution include:

- Managed accounts - This allows installation and management of accounts including access to email and calendar options. It also allows for the resetting of passwords and deletion of accounts.
- Configuration - Settings and restrictions can all be configured centrally. Passcodes and supervision are commonly adjusted here.
- App management - The MDM allows the administrator to install and manage apps. This includes pushing apps to be downloaded or the removal of apps. This can be done at a whole school, group or individual level.
- Security - The MDM has provision for passcode locking, remote wipe of data for a lost or stolen device and enforced restriction management.
- Profile Manager - A feature of an OS X server that allows the remote management of Mac and iOS devices. This makes configuration a simple process and is adaptable for each school's specific requirements.

It is worth mentioning that whichever third party MDM solution is chosen, the software within the Apple devices is developed to suit the context of a school. This means that cloud hosted and internal server solutions are compatible and also accommodates differing budgets. Free solutions like

Meraki sit alongside paid platforms such as Lightspeed, Airwatch or Casper with each offering variable levels of service.

At the time of writing, the Meraki system is free (it's web-hosted) and serves many schools adequately. The paid-for MDMs are priced per-device per-year and start at around £5, going all the way up to around £18, though for that price you get a host of add-ons which you might not need. This amounts to a lot of money overall, so this question is one which should be given just as much research and time as the consideration of case or insurance. For an 'average' school, total MDM cost for a three year scheme could be anywhere from £15,000 to £54,000, so a product would have to be seriously good to rival a totally free and largely comparable alternative. As ever, it all depends on your context and what you consider to be critical functions of the tool.

We won't attempt to compare the various products here, as this would be out of date almost instantly. Our advice is to consider what your biggest problems are (usually around deployment and managing users' access to disruptive/ inappropriate applications) and ask the suppliers to demonstrate in a live environment how their product would deal with a specific situation. In the past, MDM companies have promised the Earth but have been hampered in their attempts to deliver it by restrictions built in by the manufacturer (yes, Apple, we're looking at you - please fix the profile deletion issue!) This changes all the time, however, so do your homework and visit 1-to-1 schools using a couple of rival systems to get an unbiased opinion on how suitable the product will be for you. There's no real market leader - even looking across just the authors' schools, Airwatch, Casper, Lightspeed and Meraki are in use.

5.7.2.1 Casper

Casper, by JAMF software, bills itself as one of the most comprehensive MDM solutions on the market. As well as having its own app, that allows a teacher to control app use in the classroom, Casper provides a platform to manage mobile technology across a school. Features include:

- Configuration Profiles: Control iPad settings from Casper Suite for example: Input Wi-Fi settings, add email accounts, restrict App Store content by age, restrict certain app settings and many more;
- Apps: Send free and paid apps to iPads and allow users to download them;
- eBooks: Send eBooks to users for download, either 'in-house' created ones or ones from the iBooks Textbook store;
- Management: Allows IT to manage iPads, with an inventory of enrolled devices and the ability to wipe or remove passcodes from a user's device;
- Casper Focus app: Allow a teacher to control app use in the classroom including restricting use to one app.

5.7.2.2 *Airwatch*

Airwatch by VMWare is possibly the biggest and most popular of the MDM solutions, now owned by one of the biggest players in the technology industry. Airwatch offers a number of interesting options for schools. Like Casper, it has it's own app for taking control of student devices, but there are a lot of additional features (that come at an additional cost) that may also be of interest. Its main features are the same as the ones listed above for Casper (Airwatch call their 'focus app' Airwatch Teach and Airwatch Learn for teacher and student respectively).

On top of this, there are options to facilitate a remote view of a student device, as well as 'Secure Content Locker' which allows for the safe storage of documents and other media for access on mobile devices anywhere, anytime (if you haven't already moved to free cloud storage from GAFE or O365).

5.7.2.3 *Lightspeed*

Technical challenges for schools adopting 1-to-1 schemes include creating methods of workflow, identifying and securing web/ applications use, and simplifying device configuration (setting restrictions, publishing apps and wireless network credentials). As a complete solution few products exist but you will find many loose, dislocated answers to these problems. However, Lightspeed Systems offers a suite of integrated services to meet these challenges.

Mobile Manager: Lightspeed offers all of the standard MDM features but an additional selling point is the global proxy that ensures web filtering policies are enforced no matter the source of Internet connectivity. Rules are applied through administrator-defined groups, with the notion of policy inheritance. For this reason management is akin to an Active Directory environment. Users enrol their devices against the group applicable to them thus adopting the apps, wireless network connection, web clips and management policies.

A particularly impressive part of Lightspeed is its enrolment procedure. Users can be handed a device pre-enrolled by using Apple Configurator or the user can enrol themselves by using a URL which will is unique to that user group or user type. Other MDMs require administrative work to ensure the user's device is placed into a group reflecting the policies and resources they apply. For devices loaned to students, over-the-air control and inventory is essential, so the ability to lock and reset the device should it become lost or even generating reports to ascertain when a device last checked in is useful. You can even see which devices require update or whether app deployment was successful.

My Big Campus: My Big Campus comes free with your Lightspeed box and it's basically a Learning Management System built around the concept of social networking. The service aims to connect educators, students and their parents or guardians through a single platform. Educators assign learning objectives, collect their student's work and return assessment feedback. Students benefit from the ability to communicate with third party educators as well as their peers outside of school hours. Parents are able to monitor their children's progress. Putting its use as a communication tool aside, MBC includes tools such as cloud storage, learning materials, and a lesson organiser.

Rocket Web Filter: Unlike My Big Campus and Mobile Manager, the Lightspeed web filter is a physical appliance that bridges your local network and the Internet, with web filtering policies therefore applied to all network devices without being dependant on an installed agent. When the device connects to the network the user is prompted to authenticate using a web browser through a captive portal. Rule-sets and web filtering policies are applied based on identifying the user, who will normally belong to an Active Directory group with a rule-set applied.

The Rocket hosts a proxy system allowing filtering to be used outside the local network. There is a choice of Rockets on the market to suit your school's needs. Its more common form is the 'Bottle Rocket', a 100mbps model. Where multiple school sites or connections exist it is possible to set up the Lightspeed Rocket in a parent/ child configuration to replicate policies applied. For federated trust schools, consistency is best delivered by applying a policy once instead of manual application for each school site. For larger establishments 1gbps and 10mpbs models are available where trusts of schools rely on a single point of Internet connection. Fairly recently Lightspeed have started to offer email filtering services costed by number of managed mailboxes.

Lightspeed Rocket supports YouTube for schools, a collection of educational videos approved as safe. Educators have the power to create their own safe playlists to share with students. For My Big Campus users, educators have the ability to embed their chosen videos into assignment post, embedded media thus becoming approved. Lightspeed also utilises web zones managed by authorised staff. Web zones can be created on the fly for the purpose of a lesson, allowing the busy IT support team to devolve temporary web filtering to teaching staff. This way the lesson will go on without the educator's fear of their chosen resources being unavailable to students.

Lightspeed's services complement each other well whether it be applying the web filter through the Mobile Manager, or delivering a safe education-focused environment through the three services together.

5.7.2.4 *Meraki*

Meraki stands out from this comparison because it is absolutely free and fulfils most of the functions other paid alternatives offer, except, most notably, the ability for teachers to take control of students' devices during a lesson. The reason for this is that manufacturers (Apple in particular) place many restrictions on what MDM software can actually manage, resulting in several MDM software options with price points ranging from £0 to £18 that are virtually identical in capability and, often, even in the way they look and feel. Some of the features Meraki includes are:

- Multi-platform device management, allowing you to manage a variety of devices and operating all at the same time;
- Individual devices can be remotely locked and erased;
- Enforce policies and restrictions to defined profiles or according to device type;
- Depending on your Wi-Fi infrastructure, Meraki can push connectivity settings to devices, meaning that you do not need to rely on end users to configure settings;
- Content management for devices. Depending on the device you are using and their operating system, Meraki allows you to push and sync documents, images, apps and other files to users or groups of users in different ways.

If granular teacher control of the apps that are used in a lesson is not high on your list of priorities, then Meraki does what all the others do, only for nothing. If a school feels they need to lock down iPads every time they come out in a lesson, then we suggest this school may have problems that need to be solved at a different level, way before they get anywhere near any 1-to-1 implementations.

6 IT'S ALL ABOUT THE WORKFLOW

Workflow simply refers to the passing of content, assignments and feedback between teacher and student. It has been part of learning forever and has remained in a recognisable guise for over a hundred years, with all the drawbacks of highly inefficient paper processes. With the advent of mobile technology, workflow is changing and it is one of the more significant reasons schools are considering 1-to-1 programmes. The options set out in this chapter should help inform ecosystem and device selection to best suit a school's context and students.

The 'perfect' workflow should provide a seamless pathway between student and teacher that enables feedback and progress to be meaningful, effective and rapid. Information, content and assignments should be easily accessed anywhere, anytime. Feedback should be easy and efficient to give, and should lead to on-going, meaningful engagement with the next steps in learning. There shouldn't be any delay and the workflow should sit alongside the information a student requires to learn effectively.

To place this in context, consider a workflow where a teacher has two contact periods a week, Monday and Thursday. The 'normal' workflow would see the assignment set on the Monday, submitted on the Thursday, feedback received on the following Monday and responded to by the second Thursday. Compare this to a system which allows the submission and feedback to happen aside from contact time and that doesn't involve complicated learning platforms.

The Feedback Loop

It would be folly to suggest that this workflow example could happen for every piece of work but the point is that, if it enhances the learning process and it is appropriate, then it is now possible with minimal organisational effort. The technology provides the platform for the student and teacher to make progress with as many workflow barriers as possible removed.

Of course this isn't always possible even with the best technology and there are a number of barriers that may need to inform your workflow strategy. There could be limitations due to infrastructure. Are there delays with login? Difficulty with access outside school walls? Is it a workflow that is based on IT considerations rather than learning? Similarly, consider the limitations of stakeholders. Is the skillset of teachers suitable for a new workflow? Do students/ teachers resist change for fear of the system failing? Do they perceive that it's all too difficult?

Everyone can agree that these problems are only worth overcoming if the learning process is enhanced. Too often the quest for workflow involves workarounds and 'making do because that's what the teachers are used to'. Unless a workflow is adopted based on sound learning outcomes, it will only serve to undermine through poor time management or duplication of effort.

Consider a simple tool such as email, which is a very effective way of communicating due to its immediate delivery. It is tempting to adopt it as your workflow. After all, everyone understands it already. However, email was not designed to be a school learning workflow solution. Suggesting students should submit work via email is a classic example of creating unnecessary work for a teacher or student. Where will the work be stored? How will it be returned efficiently? How will the teacher manage every students' submissions? "Just email it to me" is not an efficient workflow solution and can be more trouble than benefit. Pretty quickly you'll discover that an email-based workflow is not an enhancement to a paper-based one, and in some respects is a backwards step.

It can also be tempting to use a tablet's full functionality within your workflow, when something simpler would be just as effective and simpler for everyone. Is video feedback worth considering? Yes. Is video feedback worth considering if the student can only access it in school? Probably not. When making decisions about workflow it should be based on the outcomes desired to support learning. If it doesn't provide timely feedback and suit the needs of the learner, what's the point?

The important thing to bear in mind is that failure to identify a suitable workflow solution(s) for students will undermine any 1-to-1 device environment. Fortunately, fairly recent developments in education technology have provided a host of options with which to tackle the workflow problem and allow time to be used more appropriately. The common thread to all of the workflow solutions suggested below is ease of submission and provision of feedback, in as few clicks as possible.

Section 6.1 Considerations for workflow

These suggested workflow options are for a variety of hardware solutions. Some are device-specific and others can be used cross-platform. There is no 'one size fits all' solution and there are many schools that adopt a number of these workflows to suit age and ability. In a fast changing environment, it is worth noting how quickly these solutions evolve. However, the basis for choice, seamless integration with the learning process, remains the same.

Teachers can be switched off by a workflow that contain more than 2-3 steps or involves switching between apps more than once, so workflow choice is very important. Thankfully, the market has developed and workflow options are becoming more streamlined and efficient. When considering these options, it is interesting to look at how schools with 1-to-1 technology have changed their approach in the last few years.

Early adopter schools in 2011/12 searched for workflow solutions that would meet the demands of their environment. Existing school applications didn't support tablet/ Chromebooks particularly well so a number of products came to the fore. Cloud-based storage options such as Dropbox were very popular alongside learning platforms such as Evernote, Edmodo or Schoology. Existing internal networks were adapted with WebDav, Securlink and Foldr offering slightly more familiar templates. The point is, early adopting schools were scrabbling for platforms to support the pedagogy and arriving at a number of different conclusions. Some of these solutions weren't particularly effective and confusion was a common theme.

Move forward to 2015 and the picture is very different. As schools have adapted to 1-to-1 technology over the years, so have the learning platforms. There are still various products available, (although it is interesting how the most appropriate are also free). However, it is much more simple to make a choice based on effective use and informed recommendation.

Chromebooks are supported by Google Apps for Education and include a workflow product called Google Classroom. This has been adopted by both 1-to-1 iPad schools and those opting for Bring Your Own Device (BYOD) as it is accessible through the Chrome browser. These 1-to-1 environments are often also supported by Edmodo, a free online learning platform, with over 13 million users that is very popular for its peer to peer collaboration component. In addition, many 1-to-1 iPad schools are using GAFE alongside iTunes U (please see section on iTunes U below) to deliver content to their learners. An iPad specific app, Showbie, has become very popular for assignment workflow with built in audio feedback. And some schools are using all of the above!

These options are popular because they support the learning process, are easily accessible and they are almost entirely free. Teachers are adopting these platforms because they ensure the workflow is as frictionless as possible and time can be spent learning rather than on logistics.

As the various advantages and disadvantages are discussed below, bear in mind that schools often opt for more than one solution to ensure the learning process is enhanced, not hindered, depending on the context of their school and the age of the students.

Section 6.2 Cloud-based Workflow

Cloud-based solutions use a network of remote servers to process, manage and store data using the Internet as the delivery mechanism. They don't require local servers in school to help with workflow. The immediate benefit is the ability to upload/ download files from any device that has an Internet connection, without needing to authenticate against the school's Windows domain. Users can also work on documents collaboratively and allow multiple people to view and/ or edit files. This removes the problems with accessing information when off school premises and the perils of multiple login, school-hosted, learning environments.

The cloud's mobility and flexibility goes hand in hand with the Chromebook/ tablet environment, leading to greater collaboration and engagement. Because the user isn't restricted by access, the cloud based solution is an enabler, improving workflow between teacher and student.

6.2.1   Cross-platform solutions

There are many cross platform solutions such as, Google Apps for Education, Dropbox, Office 365, Edmodo and Box that all serve to provide an accessible workflow environment that is hosted remotely. Some of these products offer much more than a workflow solution, for example, calendar and email integration, some are little more than online storage, whilst others are geared specifically to learning. When choosing a cloud-based solution, look for the functionality before considering cost and logistics. It may be that existing systems are no longer fit for purpose and a cloud-based solution for workflow may also contain the solution for a number of IT infrastructure concerns.

6.2.1.1 Office 365

Microsoft are a little late to the 1-to-1 party, but to make up for it they've brought a 2 litre bottle of White Lightning and a family-size bag of twiglets. Office 365 is the company's online storage and productivity-app offering, granting access to their famous Office suite, across the Internet on a variety of devices. Imagine it as a kind of Dropbox meets Word, only slightly less fun than that sounds.

To add to this, there are now separate iOS apps for each of these iconic Microsoft products, meaning that - finally! - your students can free themselves from the shackles of all that creative nonsense and get back to making some serious PowerPoints. With transitions *and* sound effects.

We'll take our tongues out of our collective cheeks at this point and give praise where it's due - the lack of Office on the iPad was actually quite a big psychological problem for many schools, IT managers and parents who saw it as a key part of a modern education and preparation for the world of work. That is now fixed. You can even make it work on a Chromebook via the web apps, but understandably Google don't shout about this option.

The fact that Office365 is free (to schools that already have an EES licence in place, and most do) and that Student Advantage allows your pupils to unlock the iOS apps is also really valuable - see Section 5.4.2 for details of this.

Here are the highlights of what you get in O365:

- Access to the Office web apps, and the desktop/ iOS apps via Student Advantage;
- 1Tb of online storage per user, now called 'OneDrive';
- Integration with the school's Active Directory;
- Hosted SharePoint for the school.

The first point has been covered above, so we won't labour this; it's either important to your school or it isn't. The 1Tb of storage is insanely huge and, because of Point 3 in the list, means that a pupil's work is both secure and in the cloud. Both these advantages are explored further in Section 5.4, but it's a good halfway house between a locked-down, on-premises traditional network and the kind of avant garde solution offered by GAFE that worries Network Managers so much. But it's the final item, the school's SharePoint instance, that can act as a workflow.

Within O365's SharePoint, authorised users can create 'sites' (e.g. 'Class 9P'), invite others to collaborate and fill them with content from their OneDrive. Teachers can add shared calendars and other content like video, a bit like Google Sites. Pupils can subscribe to be updated as documents change and can collaborate through sharing documents. There's a 'Shared with me' list of files and the ability to create shared folders. Its integration into the school's email product ties all this together and the interface is both pared down and instantly familiar.

Microsoft have also just released something called 'OneNote Class', which brings the power of OneNote into the collaborative environment of a school's O365 SharePoint. This will allow teachers to make shared notebooks for classes and individual students, creating a much smoother workflow than just SharePoint alone.

All this said, O365 doesn't *quite* convince as a 1-to-1 workflow yet, lacking the 'designed for online' feel and being a bit too serious and prone to error. Because O365 is relatively young, it's not integrated into as many apps as more established solutions like GAFE. Office 365 is more like what you'd end up with if you took an historic programme suite of incredible complexity and tried to squeeze it onto someone's phone. Which is exactly what it is. However, it's worth investigation as it's a rich offer, ties in brilliantly with the wider school network and PCs, may help nervous users transition smoothly to a new paradigm and, you never know, might eventually mature into something really useful to schools.

6.2.1.2 *Google Apps for Education*

Let's turn our attention now to one of the most popular cloud-based solutions in schools across the world, Google Apps for Education (GAFE).

Whilst nothing is ever 'free' in education, GAFE comes pretty close from a user perspective. Google bill the product as 'free Web-based email, calendar & documents for collaborative study anytime, anywhere.' With unlimited free storage given to each user, it is difficult to argue. They do impose a limit of 5Tb on individual file size. For reference, that's a 600-hour long video file, so you'll probably be able to squeeze under that ceiling. Google's commercial model is based on advertising, but no advertisement or user data collection take place within GAFE, following recent court cases in the US. Google have gone to great and public lengths to reiterate how they don't snoop on data in GAFE domains. It's free to education, some would argue, because Google want students to continue to use their services as adults. All technology companies exist to make money; it seems that Google's model of doing so has yet to reach the stage at which it is accepted without suspicion.

The component to concentrate on is Google Drive which is a user's online storage, integrated into the Google Calendar and Mail. Drive serves as an excellent example of how cloud-based storage can help the learning process, allowing the user to:

- Access files anytime on any device with an Internet connection;
- Work offline with documents;
- Share files/ documents with others and collaborate in real time;

- Share folders with students and receive and feedback on assignments;

- Allow read-only access on documents and share with students as a resource, with no photocopying;

- Save/ export a document in a variety of formats including those used by MS Office;

- Work with other Google Apps to provide a platform for forms, surveys, projects;

- Save to Google Drive with two taps of an icon or clicks of a mouse;

- Integration directly into many iPad apps;

- Search files in Drive for name or keyword.

The ease with which documents or folders can be shared should be the starting point for anyone looking to implement GAFE. Suddenly a logistical barrier to collaboration is removed and the user can see updates in real time. For example, let's look at a creative writing project. A document can be set up with a number of writing prompts for a student or group of students. The teacher grants editing access to the students and each student can view any contribution as they construct their piece. The teacher can make comments on progress or suggest changes to the content. Perhaps most importantly, the teacher can view the construction of sentences over time. The creative process is then seen as a work in progress rather than an end product. If a student often pauses mid-sentence in their writing that might lead to pertinent feedback that enhances learning for the student. Therefore witnessing the process of writing is a desirable part of the workflow that was very difficult to manage before collaborative documents.

The document also has a revision history so the teacher or student can refer to different parts of the process. This revision history also acts as a fail safe against accidentally deleted work. It may (or may not!) interest the reader to know that this book was written using a collaborative Google Doc, with the five authors working asynchronously, adding comments to each others' work, having live calls to improve the draft whilst watching the words change on their individual screens.

The collaborative folder in Drive can also work as a class resource sharing area. The teacher simply shares a folder with every member of the class and gives them 'view only' access. This means that the teacher can be comfortable that the students can access the resources without fear they might delete them. The students can work on a copied version of the resource but the master will remain secure.

To take this a step further, the folder structure can also act as a workflow solution for a single teacher and a student. A shared editable folder between the teacher and student means content and assignments can be stored and shared with access available at any time. The student simply submits an assignment to the folder and the teacher provides feedback in the form of comments on the Google Doc or annotations as appropriate. Digital annotations can be provided through a third party application such as Notability (iOS app) or Markup (Chrome Extension). The fantastic thing about this workflow is there is no grey area for assignment submission. It can't be 'lost' as editing is time stamped, as is deletion of materials. Students quickly learn that excuses aren't easily evidenced!

When considering a solution such as GAFE, the implications to shifting to an entirely new platform must be carefully thought through. GAFE offers calendar, email and storage solutions that are integrated and work as an ecosystem rather than an add-on. It's hard to use GAFE effectively unless you have fully committed to it in its entirety; it's possible (but a pretty horrible user experience) to keep your Microsoft email/ calendaring system and link it to GAFE. There is a cost implication of the move away from a product such as MS Exchange for email and Office for productivity, mostly seen in the subsequent training required. Data protection and adherence to policy should also be carefully looked at with the knowledge that other Google products allow Google to 'mine' for data so they can target advertising. Even though GAFE domains are not included in the list of products, it needs to be flagged up as a potential concern.

6.2.1.3 Google Classroom

If GAFE can be thought of as the basic building blocks of workflow, Google Classroom is the mortar that holds them together. Classroom is a workflow solution that is available as part of a Google Apps for Education domain. A relatively new product, 'Classroom' seeks to provide a platform for teachers and students to assign and turn in work using Google Drive as supporting storage.

Students are linked to a teacher's account using a unique code which is assigned when the teacher creates a class account, or the teacher can add users/ groups of users to a class themselves. Each student then has access to all announcements and assignments as the teacher posts material.

Initially the platform can be used to inform students of upcoming events or required content. However, it is most effective as an assignment workflow. The teacher titles an assignment and can describe exactly what is required. There is then the ability to attach material from a variety of sources, the most useful of which is directly from Drive. All materials are automatically copied into individual folders for each student so there is no concern that material will be incorrectly moved or deleted. It is in this individual student folder where the student will also turn-in the assignment for assessment. Again, only the student and their teacher can view this folder and can resubmit work if required. As a useful component of the process this portfolio of assignments is curated into a 'Classroom' folder which is created in Drive automatically for every individual.

Google Classroom is compatible with any Internet-enabled device as it runs through the Chrome browser. It is therefore worthy of consideration as a workflow solution regardless of chosen hardware and its simplicity makes it an excellent starting point as teachers begin to adapt to new workflows. Once a class is set up the software will continue to make individual copies of assigned material so every student is in control of their own work. This is helped by its inclusion as a GAFE product so students are likely to already be familiar with Drive.

Classroom is earmarked for major development in the coming months although it is already clear that it provides a number of opportunities to enhance learning:

- Resource sharing - any resource in Drive or from a computer can be assigned to the students, including videos and URLs;
- Individual student folders - Classroom can remove the need for large shared folders with all students added;
- Class communication - all class announcements could be made on the platform with individuals notified with updates;
- Document review - assignments can be turned in at any point with the review process allowing the teacher to accept editing after the turn in date. This works very well for essay writing;
- Email groups - Classroom allows a teacher to email every member of a group with no need for email group creation;
- Student assignment submission - Classroom keeps track of who has submitted and at what time.

There are of course limitations to Google Classroom with the option to provide audio and video feedback high on the wish list. It would also be useful to annotate with a pen tool, particularly as assignments are often media-rich in a 1-to-1 environment. However, as the process of folder creation and individual material assignment is automated it comes strongly recommended. There is always the risk with Google products that it might not be supported for many years to come, but Drive integration lessens this problem. At the end of the school year a student will have a Classroom folder in their Drive storage area with all assignments safe and secure.

A very worthy workflow contender.

6.2.1.4 Edmodo

Whilst GAFE and Office365 offer a package of services in the Cloud, there are platforms that look to solely support teaching and learning from the end user's point of view. Take Edmodo for example.

Edmodo bills itself as a 'social learning platform' for teachers, students and parents. It works on any device with an Internet connection and is a very popular workflow solution in the 1-to-1 environment:

- Students have the ability to turn-in or upload assignments that the teacher can annotate and provide feedback directly inside the app;
- Parents can login to the website to view their child's assignments or grade;
- Student or class data can be generated and made available with graphical representation;
- Peers can collaborate on the 'wall' using a Facebook-style interface to pose and answer questions;
- The website allows you to create quizzes and polls to enhance the learning process;
- Edmodo is integrated with Google Drive so content can be made available to support learning and attached to assignments, notes or polls.

Edmodo is a free, secure environment within which learning can be enhanced. Students aren't even required to use their names (if that is suitable) and access to a group is only gained through a class code. With over 30 million registered users it is clearly a platform that is popular with schools around the world. All content and data is stored on Edmodo servers (check permission base for under 13s) and access is free for all.

If you are a Lightspeed customer (see Section 5.7.2.2), the bundled My Big Campus offers a similar though more controllable/ configurable service to Edmodo and is worth considering.

6.2.2   Vendor-specific options

A number of hardware providers seek to develop loyalty by providing content solutions that are device-specific. For example, whilst Google Classroom is available through the Chrome browser, and therefore accessible cross-platform, its 'add on' software packages are released on

Google platforms before being made available elsewhere. Apple take it a stage further with solutions that can only be accessed on Apple hardware.

6.2.2.1 *iTunes U*

Apple have made iTunes U only accessible through the iOS app. As the iPad is currently the most popular tablet in education, it is worth discussing its Cloud-based content provision.

At first glance iTunes U is just a section of the iTunes store where students can download free content from schools and universities across the world. This content can be accessed through the iTunes U iOS app so is available to anyone with an iPad or iPhone. However, from a teacher-to-student point of view, the real learning potential comes from iTunes U course manager.

Teachers can construct their own courses through the app or any browser on a PC as long as the end product is viewed through the iOS app. This means that a teacher can aggregate content on any device and bring it together for students to follow. In essence, a lesson by lesson course can be put together with links to resources and assignments for students to follow across a topic, module or class year.

This resource manipulation is available to the students in real time. Consequently, if a teacher uploads a new resource to an existing course then that resource is instantly available to any existing course users. Initial benefits are obvious with a reduction in photocopying and resource manipulation. However, the real positives can be found when considering the diverse nature of any class group. The resources are always available to the students through the app, so differentiated tasks are easier to administer. If a student is struggling with the content they can access help in a structured all from within the app. Similarly, a student who needs to be stretched can be guided to tasks that will challenge their understanding with the resources to support learning available. If a lesson needs to be adapted because a group is making great progress then the workflow involved is much simpler. Similarly, any examples of student work can be uploaded to the course for reference.

iTunes U courses also serve to support absent students or those who have fallen behind. Whilst it is always desirable to meet with a student face to face, they can at least access a structured set of resources with assignments built in. Consequently, when considering a 1-to-1 tablet environment, iTunes U alone makes the iPad a strong contender.

6.2.2.2 Showbie

Showbie is an iOS app that allows teachers to assign, collect and review student work on the iPad. As with Edmodo, Showbie allows the teacher to provide feedback using annotations, text and voice notes from inside the app. If the student submits work in PDF form, all feedback and resubmission can be completed within the app which is a great organisational starting point for workflow.

Showbie makes use of the iPad's 'open in' function to allow students to submit work from thousands of different apps. Consequently, students can submit audio or video projects alongside text to express their learning. This is particularly useful when utilising the increased functionality of the iPad beyond the written word.

Showbie is an excellent example of how workflow can look inside a 1-to-1 classroom and helps with the concept of the paperless classroom:

- Creation of a class inside Showbie provides a unique code so students can join without the need for the teacher to register every student;
- Documents and instructions can be added to an assignment to help with student learning;
- Students receive notifications when assignments have been updated or materials changed;

- Assignment folders ensure the student remains organised and all content is stored in the cloud so if a device is lost a student can login on the new device and all their work is available;
- Students can pose questions to the teacher alongside their assignments and also record audio notes to express themselves;
- The app keeps track of the students who have submitted work and those pending.

Although Showbie is specific to iPad, it is worth referencing as a workflow for any 1-to-1 environment. The key aspects of organisation, deadline submission and stored work are covered and reduce a number of barriers to learning a typical classroom might see. The free version of Showbie is used by thousands of schools with the optional 'pro' account available for increased audio notes and functionality. The pro account offers longer voice notes, larger video upload and greater in-app annotations. Quotes can be accessed on a school by school basis here https://plans.showbie.com/schools/ . The free version has more than enough functionality for a number of teachers to trial the platform before a school decides to opt for a paid plan.

6.2.3   Limitations of cloud-based workflow solutions

Cloud-based workflow should be top of the list for consideration when implementing a 1-to-1 device scheme. However, as with all solutions, there are a number of limitations worth considering:

- The folder workflow requires Internet access, which certainly isn't available to all students at home. One solution is to provide access to the Internet before and after school so the student can store and submit changes. Documents can be worked on offline and then saved into the appropriate area as soon as the device connects with the Internet;
- Teacher understanding, training and support can be resource- and time-constrained, leading to a less than desirable implementation;
- There are privacy and security issues to consider. Does the storage of data in the Cloud meet with your school/ LA policy? Where will

the data be stored and does it lead to data protection concerns? Check that the data is going to be stored within the EU, or that the provider is a signatory of the US/EU Safe Harbour agreement;

- Dependency on the vendor: will the third party providing the product maintain the systems over time? How difficult will it be to switch providers if required? This is a particular concern with proprietary systems.

Despite this long list of limitations and worries it is worth noting that many large corporations run Cloud-based solutions for their company finances and other data. The user base continues to grow in education and business because the advantages outweigh the disadvantages. Care should be taken when selecting a product, be it GAFE, Office365 or any other education solution. However, workflow, sharing and collaboration should be uppermost in the mind when the decision is being made for teaching and learning.

Section 6.3 In-House Solutions

6.3.1   VLEs

The concept of the VLE has changed over time with a number of products adapting to the tablet market. As described in the cloud-based section, the VLE can now exist entirely in the cloud. However, this might not be desirable for a school, so in-house options may be considered.

This does of course rule out Chromebooks and Google Apps for Education as this is a cloud-based system that works through a browser. Similarly, iTunes U, Edmodo, Showbie etc all run in the cloud. The in-house VLEs store all data on the school's own servers and maintain all privacy and security settings. Much like on-premises email provision, all data remains on site and allows the school to control all settings.

The benefits of a networked VLE are much the same as the cloud based solutions:

- Content provision and curation;
- Assignment submission and feedback;
- Data tracking and representation;
- Discussion forum provision;
- Access available to all stakeholders if required, parents, teachers and students.

There are also a number of problems that come with running a network VLE and these are concerns many teachers have been expressing before the 1-to-1 environment became popular:

- Often complicated to use with a less than intuitive interface;
- Repeated login issues particularly when accessing the school site from outside the network;
- Must be maintained by in-house staff and regularly backed up;
- VLE management often falls to IT staff reducing the time available for other projects.
- Generally cost a lot to license compared to 'free' cloud-based counterparts.

In essence, they've routinely and repeatedly failed in schools because they tend to be clunky, have poor functionality and look very much like something from the 1990s. Do you really want to hang your carefully planned, exquisitely deployed and expensively bought 1-to-1 project off something as flawed as your school's VLE? Remember, workflow is the daily interaction that every student and teacher will have with 1-to-1. If in-house data storage is important then correct resourcing of the project is a must for it to succeed.

6.3.2   WebDav

WebDAV is an extension to the HTTP protocol, a web technology. WebDAV was originally intended to be the method to create and manage web documents in a collaborative nature. One document would be developed through contribution by many. A good example of this type of document is Wikipedia. Unsurprisingly. many of the web pages we see are in a read only state for our eyes however the likelihood is that what you are reading evolves from a number of third parties. Version control is a key part of the WebDAV standard ensuring the most recent contributions or amendments take precedence. You might be asking what this has got to do with 1-to-1... Many applications such as the iWork suite support WebDAV, it is a means of sharing your files between devices. There are other services such as Dropbox and Box but the difference is WebDAV is not a cloud-hosted service. Data is retained on your school's server and the owners' devices. If your technical team is up to it, they may be able to set up WebDav to allow users' data to move between your servers and a mobile device, but it's an aging technology and is far from intuitive for users.

Section 6.4 Concluding thoughts on workflow

In an ideal world, a teacher and student would sit down face to face and discuss every piece of work to ensure the student understands the next steps required to enhance their learning. Whilst this workflow would be ideal, it isn't practical, so the next best solution is to have assignment submission and feedback as seamless as possible for everyone.

Teachers now have the ability to receive assignments and provide feedback that can be accessed by the student as soon as it is submitted. Students no longer have to wait for the next contact period to receive feedback and the method has been expanded to include audio and video. This only works in a 1-to-1 environment if the right tools are selected for the context of the school and its learners. Cloud-based solutions are very popular alongside apps that ensure the teacher can provide meaningful feedback in the time available.

7 ACHIEVING SUSTAINABLE CHANGE

Section 7.1 Change Management with staff

'Change Management' is consultant speak for making your project work at the human level. The specific humans we're talking about are teachers. This is probably the greatest challenge to the successful implementation of a 1-to-1 programme:

- Helping staff with everything from how to use the device to changing their pedagogy is both resource-draining and time-consuming;
- A group of teachers being introduced to new technology for the first time are quite possibly in need of greater differentiation than any class of students;
- Users' needs can vary from an inability to turn a machine on, all the way up to problem solving a new application.

How you manage this process of change will determine how successful your project is, ultimately; plenty of 1-to-1s have failed to 'take' in schools regardless of their technical or educational quality, because of a failure to change how teachers do things.

What follows is a list of recommendations from the perspective of an iPad roll-out to staff, with class sets available to some students, but most of the ideas which follow will map directly onto any project. These tips are borne out of a desire to help teachers without overwhelming them, and to model good practice to students. There are many apps that could have been chosen to illustrate the point, but those mentioned below are considered generic and able to serve a purpose across the curriculum.

7.1.1 Get backing from the people that count

The first and most important element of any introduction of change is the full support of the leadership team. Ideally, the drive for 1-to-1 will have come directly from the Headteacher, but if not their sponsorship will emphasise the importance of this whole school initiative. A 1-to-1 programme will have an effect on pedagogy, behaviour management and finances, so buy-in from every senior stakeholder is crucial. Take any opportunity to keep them up to date with progress and to make them part of decision making. Use early-adopting teachers and groups of students to evangelise and demonstrate. Have a 1-to-1 professional development target mandated for the whole staff. Get the head to publicly and repeatedly back what you are doing so that all staff feel the weight of the message; this isn't something that is going to go away.

You will be grateful further down the track, when priority for your school's highly-prized training time remains with the project long after the lustre has worn off. The training element of this change is enormous and SLTs need to commit a substantial amount of teachers' time for the year or so it takes to embed the project. They will never do this if they don't believe in its impact. Equally, if teachers perceive that this is just another 'IT' thing rather than the vision of the school's leaders, change is unlikely to be far reaching. This latter point is crucial because many teachers will view any attempt to integrate technology as *yet-another-thing-to-do*. Another intervention. Many might not immediately appreciate that technology integration will eventually work in their favour when marking is made lighter and giving effective feedback is made easier, or when lesson planning and content delivery are enhanced and augmented.

It goes without saying that the role of 'Director of Technology' or similar is an essential part of a successful leadership formula. Someone senior, confident and with a joined-up understanding of technology and education needs to own the project and set the pace. Boundless patience and infinite positivity are also very desirable attributes for a person in this role. Please see Section 3.1 for more details. Deep, sustained change does not take place by accident or in the margins - someone needs to drive it.

7.1.2   Give staff a head-start through early familiarity

It is imperative that staff get to use the device to familiarise themselves with the potential for learning. This is no easy feat and will test whoever is leading staff training and management. One of the best things you can do to help teachers adapt is to get devices into their hands well before students start arriving with them in lessons - perhaps as soon as a year before, six months at the least. The University of Hull's 2012 study[34] showed that the individual possession of and early familiarisation with the iPad by teachers was seen as being responsible for the significant 'buy in' and low level of resistance from teachers in the six schools it looked at.

Early engagement with the technology can be facilitated by linking email accounts to the iPad and suggesting users sign up to apps like Flipboard or for a national newspaper. Interest in the content means that basic gestures on the device will be used. Sharing of information helps to introduce the options available to users and when coupled with the camera roll, can lead to greater understanding of 'sharing' options. Many schools issue teachers with devices just before a holiday, so that they can familiarise themselves with its basic operation over a few weeks, using it for basic non-work activities.

This is all common sense, but it's worrying how often teachers first get introduced to technology at the same time as the children they're supposed to be teaching with it. How would you help a frightened non-swimmer learn to stay afloat? Not by throwing them in the deep end and then getting frustrated at their panicked screams of terror...

---

[34] Burden, K. et al. (2012) iPad Scotland Evaluation. Hull: University of Hull

We won't repeat the advice in Section 3.2.2 (Piloting) on setting up departmental champions here, save to say it's a vital step in kick-starting change among staff and building engines of change within those tight-knit subject units. A good departmental champion, through the power of peer support and a little bit of healthy competition, can make a bastion of resistance into a beacon of excellence and can-do innovation.

7.1.3   Dispelling fears through leadership

Many teachers are frightened by the onrushing tsunami of change that 1-to-1 will bring to their classrooms. If it's not the erosion of their lifelong status of omnipotent expert thanks to their pupils' sudden ability to Google the hell out of anything they say, it's the tablet's role as a technological Swiss Army Knife for every disruptor, bully or ne'er-do-well in the school that really puts the willies up them.

But there are ways to help make this less frightening, because in reality, the change is overwhelmingly positive in schools that embrace rather than run from it. For example, it is crucial to model good practice particularly when the distraction element of the device is a concern. Whenever iPads are used with students there are different levels of instruction to ensure the device remains a tool for learning. From 'screens off', to 'cases closed', these instructions should also be followed throughout any staff training sessions. In particular, it is important they are used with other staff in the room so classroom management has a common strand for the students to follow. The fact that some teachers are appallingly behaved in training sessions is an advantage here, presenting you with a great opportunity to (humorously) demonstrate the behaviour management techniques they'll need to get to grips with.

Similarly, if a student doesn't follow an instruction, a consistent approach is required when dealing with them and their device. One of the biggest fears for staff is that the device will be used inappropriately, disrupting their lessons and undermining their authority. Ensuring classroom management provision are included in the Acceptable Use Policy is one way to make sure educators have common and easily understood frame of reference.

Teachers should certainly be heavily involved in the evolution of the AUP and should never feel disempowered by the use of devices in their classroom. They are still the adult and the learning tools in the room, be they iPads or pencils, must be used appropriately within a framework of rules.

Your MDM can help here too. You *should* be locking down certain elements of the ecosystem if they don't have a legitimate educational use at that moment. Remember, most MDMs are capable of geo-fencing or timed blocking, so disabling Snapchat 8am-4pm isn't the same as taking away a student's freedom to use the device socially. It's a tightrope that you'll have to walk - convincing adults that things are safe, whilst still allowing children the measure of freedom they will want to fulfil their side of the bargain (charging the device and bringing it in).

Provide a mechanism for teachers to flag things that are concerning them, freely and without fear of being seen as oppositional. When you block something technically, or remove a pupil's device privileges, let the staffroom know. Don't be afraid to stand up for a good old-fashioned 'Not in my school' approach if you think it will win over those that are wavering due to behaviour management fears.

The final tip for dispelling fear is to put your head into the lion's mouth and look happy while you're doing it. Invite teachers to observe your teaching with devices and work hard to include your 'hard to reach' colleagues. What's more, don't use your top-set Year 7 for this, pick one of your more challenging classes. By demonstrating that even you (!) can cope with disruption and the shift of the power dynamic, others will see that the things they are worried about can be overcome.

7.1.4   Enhance current pedagogy, don't trash it

A key component in helping teachers to get on board with this change is demonstrating that the device can enhance current practice, not just replicate it and not replace it with something entirely new. If you can demonstrate that this technology is going to make their teaching more effective and more efficient, without necessarily throwing the baby out with the bathwater, what is there to resist or fear? Make it relevant; it is a good idea to choose apps that can be used for collaboration, Assessment for Learning and workflow. Suggestions include Socrative for AfL, Explain Everything for collaboration and Edmodo for workflow.

It is very easy to wow an audience with what an iPad can do in the classroom but that leads to a 'show' with no follow-up. The nuanced applications that have an element of awe and wonder tend to have a very short shelf life when it comes to the classroom. Indeed a number of subject-specific apps are only suitable for use once or twice a year. Therefore it is better to demonstrate those apps that will make a difference to workload and effectiveness of both teacher and learner. Put another way, staff need to understand how Google Drive will work to share information with students or Edmodo will allow them to annotate and grade assignments without paper. They don't necessarily need to see the amazing Solar Walk or Aurasma just yet.

A decent teacher planning tool like iDoceo can win over the hardest hearts. After all, which teacher doesn't feel a slight thrill at the thought of an impeccably neat, well-ordered and colourful markbook-cum-classroom toolkit? The ability to fiddle endlessly with seating plans and keep meticulous notes on individuals' needs is a sturdy shield against the threat of the Inspector and is also valued highly.

Similarly, getting the school's MIS to be accessible through the device is an important step. If teachers need to use a PC to take the register, they may not turn on the tablet all lesson. However, if they can do it from the doorway, as the students enter, they are already integrating the iPad into a their practice and injecting a little pace into the lesson from the start. There are some great apps for this - Groupcall Emerge for SIMs is excellent.

iMovie is well worth incorporating into any training programme as the level of effort students put into such projects is unsurpassed and the results are usually very edifying, despite how ridiculously easy to use it is. It is also worth noting that any work that will be shared with 'the world' always focuses the mind of a student. The fact that an iMovie project is likely to be shown to a class means students take greater pride in making sure content is correct.

Notability is an excellent app to demonstrate how learners can work in a way they and their teacher will recognise, but on an iPad. Acting as an interactive exercise book, Notability has many features that the students and staff will become comfortable with. However, the initial reaction is always one of transitional understanding as the workflow seems comparable, apart from the lack of paper!

Finally, a great eTextbook solution can be a powerful bridge from 'old' to 'new' methods. We all know the weaknesses of paper textbooks (which include, but are not limited to, unimaginative phallic graffiti) but if your eTextbook of choice can give access to up-to-the-minute information, the ability to scribble notes in the margin without fear of detention, a way to share questions of findings between peers and other features like self-marking tests, the battle for hearts and minds will be all but won.

7.1.5   Get the Workflow right (and keep it simple)

The centrality of your chosen workflow to teachers' lives is a point worth returning to. For example, show them how easy and quick it is to give effective feedback individuals using voice or text comments in an app like Showbie. The lightbulb moment when they see how much better this is than the drawn-out and rarely impactful process of paper marking is Change Management you can almost reach out and touch. It is particularly satisfying when staff realise that students can no longer make the excuse of printer problems!

There are a number of options available to schools that allow for collection and assessment of work and these are dealt with in full elsewhere. They cater for a mixed platform environment as well as 1-to-1 iPads. The key is to remove any barriers to the initial setup. Spend time linking iPads to individuals' Google Drive accounts (or whatever cloud storage you've gone for) and trialling the interaction between stakeholders in a room full of trouble-shooters.

7.1.6   Use Digital Leaders to ease the transition

Technology goes wrong a lot, that's why teachers don't trust it. On top of this, teachers can feel pressure to be knowledgeable about technology, the only seeming alternative to this being to withdraw from the arena entirely. With this in mind, each class will benefit hugely from its own technical experts who will be able to troubleshoot for teachers and students alike. Staff will be very thankful that there are three or four individuals who are able to help with the technology in the classroom and won't care that they are twelve years old. The 'safety net' that Digital Leaders can provide is invaluable and it might make teachers more prepared to try something new. It is worth remembering that, once an individual gets to grips with the iPad interface, many applications have a similar functionality, but many teachers won't reach this stage of familiarity without help. Even though the above example is for the beginnings of an iPad 1-to-1 programme, the same principles apply for any device; see section 8.2 below for a detailed look at how to set up a Digital Leaders programme.

7.1.7   Training - Champions, CPD, Coaching

Without effective training and support, any teacher will struggle to progress alongside all the other school commitments they have. As was mentioned in Section 3.2, a full training programme requires detailed planning and significant free capacity, at least a 0.5 FTE timetable devoted to this. This is because the training, coaching and in-class support needed should be spread out over months, a regular drip-drip of help, advice and skills input rather than a couple of intensive days' training and it should be available 'on demand', not at fixed times.

The school's early adopters should become part of the training programme and if at all possible every department should have a technology champion so staff have regular access to support. These champions can lighten the load for any Director of Technology and can be more effective, as their context is so similar to the people they're helping. This is also dealt with in Section 3.1 above.

One of the challenges is understanding the actual training needs of your colleagues. Some may present as vaguely competent and actually have very little idea of how to use devices to support learning, and equally some may hide under a bushel a deep and valuable understanding and set of skills. Unless your staff is small and stable, it's likely that you won't have the in-depth knowledge you need to design a training programme that meets everyone's needs. For this, a Training Needs Analysis (TNA) tool is required. It serves a number of purposes:

- to identify those most in need of intensive support;
- to identify those who might be able to support others, particularly in specific areas of expertise;
- to help you plan large-scale training aimed at common areas of weakness/ concern;
- to help you plan training targeted at smaller groups (e.g. the English department), based on a better understanding of their skills.

The best way to administer the TNA is via an online survey and the best way to analyse responses is via a spreadsheet.

Some people will need really intensive support and you will need to make a judgement about who should get your time and what constitutes 'enough' progress for this term/ year. Equally, some teachers will resist the change, whatever you do to support them. This is something that many 1-to-1 leaders struggle with, pouring time and energy into trying to shift the most stubborn of refuseniks. Our advice? Put your effort where it is likely to have an outcome and 'ignore the haters'. If you can create momentum with 75% of staff, they may carry the rest with them. Those who still won't engage in the face of whole-school adoption wouldn't be any different if you spent several days time chipping away at their obstinacy. Teach to the top end.

7.1.8   Change Management for Staff - Top Tips

So, to summarise:

- Full support of Leadership team with regular communication;
- A defined Director of Technology role for implementation;
- Regular training sessions with support available by email, in lessons and 1-to-1;
- Model good practice and offer lesson observations;
- Implement a student Digital Leader programme;
- Identify a staff technology champion in every department;
- Remember that use of the technology is always about learning not the device;
- Find quick wins that make the change worthwhile for staff;
- Focus your time on the positives.

Section 7.2 Change Management with pupils

7.2.1   Digital Leaders

One of the most transformative components of a successful 1-to-1 programme is free, available in every classroom and keen to learn. That component is the student body, or more importantly, those willing to act as Digital Leaders. Such is the success of Digital Leader programmes throughout the UK that there is a nationwide framework of Digital Leaders sharing tips and resources. Contact can be made through the Digital Leader network that can be found at www.digitalleadernetwork.co.uk Highly recommended as a starting point for research and collaboration.

Whilst the concept of handing over responsibility might be difficult for some staff, it is crucial that they embrace the help students can offer when using technology in the classroom. Indeed, many staff will be fearful of technology full-stop, so having a trained, trusted and knowledgeable set of helpers in the classroom can relieve teachers of this psychological load. They don't need to understand how it all works, they just need to understand why it is useful for learning.

A teacher should be supporting the learning process and not have to deal with any user issues with technology. Chromebooks and iPads are very robust as tools for learning. However, the same cannot always be said of the user. Failure to update apps or remember simple workflows are a headache for any 1-to-1 programme coordinator. The onus should not be on the teacher in the classroom to troubleshoot these issues. Likewise the IT team don't need to babysit the students as they use the device. Step forward Digital Leaders and the wealth of knowledge and support they can bring to a 1-to-1 programme.

The aim is to provide a teacher with the ability to say to a student 'if you're having an issue with that application, speak to our wonderful Digital Leaders when I've finished explaining what we're going to do'. Whilst this may sound idealistic, programmes like this have been used for decades in schools. Whether it is representatives for school council, milk monitors or library duty, students are very good at taking on roles of responsibility. The key is to manage the start-up and training process in such a way that the Digital Leaders are almost self sufficient with a little support from staff.

Thankfully students are curious. Without this curiosity, a Digital Leader programme wouldn't be so successful. Show them something they are interested in and they want to know more. If they come up against a barrier, they want to overcome it. If they can find out something no-one else knows, they want to share it. Successful Digital Leaders are the epitome of the curious student with more to offer schools than perhaps any other student body at this time. The classroom environment is changing and students and teachers need their help.

Aspects to consider are:

Digital Leader Responsibilities:

- A guide when using technology to support learning;
- Exponent of new and existing applications;
- Trainer and supporter of school members including parental, teacher and student bodies.

The example below is taken from a 1-to-1 iPad initiative which serves to illustrate how crucial Digital Leaders are to the success of any roll-out. It must be emphasised that the roles and responsibilities are transferable to any technology in schools.

Digital Leader Model:

- An iGenius in each class (responsible for communication with students and teachers alike);
- Four further Digital Leaders in each class;
- Genius Bar run every lunchtime (in a very public space);
- Training given once a week to Digital Leaders to support their development;
- Edmodo group for communication, sharing good practice and new ideas.

Selection:

- Students submit a 30 second presentation to a panel of interviewers. The presentation can involve any application although the most common is an iMovie with different apps used to create the content;
- The panel then ask questions centred around communication and commitment. An ability to understand that skill levels are varied is key to the selection process, alongside communication skills;
- Digital Leaders chosen to meet the model requirements (with respect given to outstanding candidates above and beyond the four Digital Leaders per class).

Training:

- First to receive information about new apps/ ideas;
- Lunchtime training for selected Digital Leaders based on focus for the week ahead. This allows for weekend interaction and feedback amongst the group. Training includes appropriate digital communication and presentation suggestions;
- Access to key information from the teaching body and IT support;
- Consistent rewards for attendance and application – in line with school achievement policy/

Practicalities:

- The primary aim of the Digital Leader programme is to support learning in the classroom;
- The presence of four 'experts' in the classroom means a teacher should never have to deal with technological issues – Wi-Fi, App use, Workflow etc. The reality is that the Digital Leaders provide a safety net without having to call a member of the IT support team. Consequently, teachers are more likely to try new applications knowing the Digital Leaders are trained to support them
- A teacher needs to manage when the Digital Leaders can offer support and ensure it doesn't hinder their own learning
- Feedback and praise works very well in the iPad environment as it can be shared instantly. For example, the Edmodo group serves as an excellent way of highlighting contributions
- The Genius Bar, run by an iGenius and four Digital Leaders, must serve to solve issues for any school member. It helps to have a focus that the Digital Leaders can demonstrate to encourage interaction. Set up is easy as everything is wireless!
- The presence of four or five Digital Leaders in each class means that absence or forgetfulness is barely noticed. If in doubt, more is definitely more

Examples of Success:

- GAFE sign up for new students was as simple as asking the Digital Leaders to ensure all members of their class had an account;
- A question from a teacher posted on the Edmodo 'wall' led to fifteen responses with answers to the query. As a result an app was 'gifted' to all students that hadn't been previously used;
- A Digital Leader came up with a method of downloading any file from the Internet into the Goodreader app that meant it was a one step process to transfer files (including from existing VLE);
- If the Digital Leaders have an issue they communicate with each other, via Edmodo, discover the answer and thank anyone that

helped for their time. As a consequence their 'chatroom' will be used a as a model of good practice

The reality is, it is difficult to see how a 1-to-1 programme could be properly supported without Digital Leaders in the classroom. There isn't the funding or manpower to support all teachers and students and fellow students are better equipped in many situations. There is a time commitment to the process and the initial setup is crucial to success. However, it is worth it and the payback for all the questions that don't have to be answered cannot be underestimated!

One last tip - train Digital Leaders to be masters of workflow. Fellow teachers will be grateful.

Engaging so many of the student body in the Digital Leader programme will help to engage sceptical students with technology use. The device should only be used to enhance learning and as such requires that students don't feel uncomfortable using it. With four or five leaders in each classroom, it quickly becomes the norm to help fellow students with any issues and this speeds up device adoption. Fortunately, the hardware is now much more intuitive to use so problems are often simple to solve. This also means that when a student asks for IT support it is more likely to be a technical issue rather than a user issue. This allows the IT team to concentrate on the infrastructure rather than troubleshooting.

Digital Leaders are a fantastic resource throughout a 1-to-1 device rollout and beyond. Engage and train those chosen and the fruits of your early labour will be clear to all.

7.2.2   Acceptable Use Policies

Schools in the pre-1-to-1 stage can fall into the trap of worrying incessantly about pupils' behaviour with the devices they are about to issue. The default position seems to be to try and lock the things down to an extent that many features are unusable. There are even schools who have disabled, at the hardware level, the built-in camera of their 1-to-1 devices, for fear of what the children would photograph and then distribute. This is despite the fact that many of the reasons they chose that device in the first place centred around the fluidity with which it could integrate still and moving images with words and sound.

What invariably happens in these situations is that human ingenuity finds a way past any impassive and mechanistic restriction. They jailbreak the device, remove the MDM profile, connect via their phone's 3G to circumvent Internet filters, et cetera.

Whatever technical solution you impose will, at some level, ultimately prove inadequate. However, there is an easier, cheaper and better way and it's through the subtler levers of education and management of people, rather than the rubber sledgehammer approach.

This should take the form of a clear framework of mutually acceptable rules by which everyone can live, normally referred to as an Acceptable Use Policy (AUP). Most schools devise a slightly more imaginative name than that though.

Teachers need the reassurance of an AUP, and one which is linked to the school's discipline policy, to feel reassured that any disruption introduced by this major change can be dealt with without ambiguity.

Pupils, bizarre as it may seem, welcome the structure and certainty of knowing what they should and should not do with their personal device when in lessons. It's easy to overlook the fact that this is just as alien experience to them as it is to the adults.

Pupils should also be heavily involved in the construction of any AUP. Humans are pretty similar in their reaction to authority - if you impose rules that tell them what to do, they tend to resist and undermine them. If they create the rules and can see why they exist, they tend to support and comply with them.

A common approach taken is to use your Digital Leaders (see Section 7.2.1) as a focus group, discussing with them the management problems and safety risks that the devices pose and letting them suggest fair and workable rules to keep everyone safe and on-task in lessons. They can also report these back to their classmates, or brief the school through an assembly. The important points are that the AUP is informed by students' views and that this is seen to have been the case by the student body.

In our experience, asking children to come up with their own rules and the sanctions for breaking them can result in an AUP that reads as if it were written by Vlad the Impaler whilst under the influence of a particularly savage hangover. Pupils' have a view that justice should be pure, swift and unforgiving, so their rules might need a little toning down.

Primarily the school AUP for mobile technology will fall into line with all other school policies. Legal requirements and terminology will be enhanced by a 'cause and consequence' model that will support parents and teachers when device use is inappropriate.

The AUP should cover all mobile technology in school, including permitted phone use if appropriate. However, it should also allow for any teacher to set additional requirements in their own classroom. This allows for practical subjects to enforce extra safeguards without the need to make the school AUP more complicated.

From a legal point of view it is important to set out 'prohibited use' and this should be continually reviewed. This list of example suggestions should be referred to your school policy on restricted content:

- Students and staff are not permitted to access, send or distribute sexually explicit, threatening, obscene, offensive or illegal materials;
- The camera or microphone must only be used with the express permission of the subject and must not be used to offend in any way;
- Copyright material is not permitted for download unless purchased by the school;
- Posting of material to the Internet is forbidden unless deemed part of the learning process by the teacher;

- The device may not be used in school changing rooms or toilets under any circumstances;
- Jailbreaking a school device is not permitted;
- The school reserves the right to search a school-owned device to ensure the AUP is adhered to.

From a user point of view the school need to be clear about non-negotiable acceptable use from the outset. This should range from simple device protection through to accessing material. For example:

- The device must remain in its protective case at all times;
- Store the device in an appropriate place, not near unstable objects or underneath other items;
- The device may not be left unattended in a vehicle;
- Only use the cleaning solution provided on the device screen;
- The device must be handed over at the request of a teacher and be available for monitoring by the school Mobile Device Management solution;
- Internet use will be monitored;
- Your password should remain secret at all times.

The AUP should also reference the device as a tool for learning:

- Only school deployed applications are permitted for download (if required);
- Ensure your cloud backup solution remains on;
- The device must be fully charged for the start of the school day;
- The device should be with you in lessons or inside your locker throughout the school day. It is not to be left unattended;
- Any device found unattended should be handed in to the IT department or nearest member of staff immediately;
- If the device is lost or stolen it should be reported immediately to your pastoral leader, IT coordinator, Headteacher.

The AUP can also be used to provide guidelines for students that can be referred to by teachers:

- If a student breaches the AUP they may be subject to removal of content from the device, confiscation of the device for a period of time, school disciplinary procedures and, if required, referred to outside agencies in the case of illegal activity;
- If a device is left at home, uncharged or confiscated, it is the responsibility of the student to complete all learning tasks;
- Any technical issues should be reported to the IT team immediately. It is still the responsibility of the student to complete all learning activities;
- The device may only be used inside the classroom or other designated areas of study;
- The device may not be used in school corridors, playground or dining hall unless authorised by a teacher.

As with any school policy the students and staff should sign the document so they agree to abide by the AUP terms. It can be very useful to get parents to countersign the AUP to help the family discuss usage at home. Schools may wish to include some guidelines for parents to follow that could also be part of the AUP if it fits with the school's policy making. For example:

- The device may only access content through home and school Internet filters;
- The device is not permitted in the bedroom unless this is a designated place of study;
- The device will charge overnight in its designated charging station away from the bedroom;
- The device should be surrendered if required by a teacher of parent to ensure it fulfils the requirement of the AUP.

This aspect of the AUP can be very helpful to teachers and parents when discussing how to manage inappropriate use. It also provides clarity and consistency when stakeholders are dealing with acceptable use.

One last thing worth mentioning is the importance of consistent sanctions for teachers to adhere to. This may or may not be part of the AUP document but could be an addition to the school behaviour policy. Suggestions include:

- Students should have the device in their bag, closed or open on their desk as directed by a teacher;
- Failure to follow classroom etiquette will result in confiscation of the device;
- After an initial warning, first time offenders will have the device confiscated until the end of the day;
- Second time offenders will have it confiscated until the parent collects the device from the pastoral leader;
- Third time offenders will be asked to attend a meeting between a Senior Leader and parent to discuss permitted use of a device for learning.

Obviously these sanctions should fall into line with the existing behaviour management strategy and an inconsistent approach can lead to real problems for teachers in the classroom, undermining the effectiveness of the device as a learning tool. As with any behaviour management strategy, whole school buy-in is crucial. When deciding on your school's sanctions, ensure they are right for your context and there are as few grey areas as possible. As the majority of students want to keep hold of their device, it's remarkable how effective the sanctions can be if enforced appropriately.

Section 7.3 Change Management with parents

7.3.1   Getting the parental body on board

If you can get parents fully behind what you are trying to do, your project will have gained vital momentum and will ultimately be more sustainable. However, this is quite a task. A campaign of information, events and – let's be honest here – pupil-powered pestering is needed and even then, there will be some tough points. The key is to get the tone right and to always lead with the educational reasons why the school is doing this.

Parents will be justifiably nervous about this project, because it affects their child's education profoundly, whether it succeeds or fails. A clear communications plan will help to ameliorate their concerns.

It's a good idea to float the concept as early as you can, and repeat the message regularly, in newsletters, at parents' evenings and prize-givings, student assemblies, through the website and VLE. This way you minimize the number of people who complain that they didn't know what was going on (though we're not sure it's possible to eliminate this entirely).

The earlier you can confirm your decision on device type the better too, as parents can become annoyed if you announce in January that you're running a 1-to-1 with, say, Windows Surface tablets and they've just bought their child the same at Christmas. An admittedly unlikely scenario, but you take our point.

It is tempting to wait and wait and see if a new killer device hits the market, but experience has taught the following two important lessons;

- Newly released devices are rarely cheap and, with a deadening regularity, ship a little bit broken (e.g. the battery is poor, or screen lags). Verdict: v1.0 of anything is usually sub-optimal, so don't hang your 1-to-1 scheme off of something untested by the brutal forces of the market. Nothing will sink your project more quickly than a poorly chosen device that the pupils hate, because their parents will quickly stop paying for them.
- Apple usually release a new iPad in the Autumn, creating a wave of publicity that the canny 1-to-1 leader can surf all the way to the beach.

The crux of your campaign will be a special information evening for parents to introduce the detail of the scheme. Having planned and run many such events, here are our top tips for success:

- Leave a slideshow running as the hall fills up with the most frequently asked (or worried about) questions and the answers to them. This will suck up a great deal of the otherwise time-consuming mollification of parents' worries at the end;

- Have the Headteacher/ Principal open the evening by describing, at a high-level if necessary, how important this scheme is to achieving the schools' educational ambitions. This is a good idea for many reasons:
    - Firstly, every parent knows who the Head is. They trust their judgment and understand that if they are backing this, then it must be important. The school is fully committed to this project, and for the right reasons. All will be well;
    - Secondly, it sets the tone from the start that this is an educational rather than a technical project. It's about learning, not devices. Make sure the Head's input hammers this message home. Craft a metaphor such as the 'bicycle for the mind' one that Steve Jobs made famous. If we know anything about Heads, it's that they love metaphors;
    - Finally, and rather sneakily, it will serve as a public commitment by the Head to back the project. If times get hard further down the line and you're fighting for funding, for CPD time or against a staff room insurgency, you can point your Headteacher to the things they told the parents at the outset. The subtle 1-to-1 leader will frequently pepper staff meetings and CPD events with references to the Head's clarity of vision and strident commitment to the project as demonstrated at the parents' event.
- Have the supplier bring someone fairly high-up from the chosen device or OS manufacturer (Apple, Google or Microsoft, most likely) to speak about the global picture of 1-to-1 schooling and, as a bye-product of this, how advanced your school is in embracing the challenge of preparing the parents' children for an uncertain, but certainly digital, future. Limit the time they have to speak and ensure to agree their focus, as this part of the evening is the bit you have least control over and can be done appallingly badly. Apple and Google are legendarily secretive about their slide sets and probably won't share them in advance, but arrange for them to arrive two hours early and run through their presentation with

them. We guarantee it will be better, shorter and more relevant to your context if you do so;

- You, as the leader of the project, should probably speak to go through some of the mechanics of the scheme;
- Having got these necessary but somewhat dry matters out of the way in the first 30 minutes, have the rest of the event a bit more hands-on and fun:
    - Teachers and pupils demonstrating how the tech helps (assessment and choice are two good themes, respectively);
    - Hands-on sessions for parents to have a go/ see devices in use in various contexts, with strong teacher champions/ selected pupils;
- Mop-up session to address parental concerns. Involve all the speakers, have a range of technical and educational people there. Expect the following parent types:
    - 85% will be people who have genuine worries about security, digital and physical. Your presentations should have addressed some of this, but it's worth spending time listening and addressing their concerns;
    - 5% will be those who think it's a con of some sort. They'll want to examine the T&Cs of the insurance line by line;
    - 5% will be the anti-Apple/ Android/ Windows8 brigade. Whatever OS you've picked, it was the wrong choice for the following 917 reasons... They usually have a semi-technical background and they'll want to talk to you for hours, before eventually agreeing to take part in the scheme;
    - 5% will be the anti-technology-in-general brigade. They'll talk about handwriting, having to write at length in exams, the danger of too much screen time and the insidiousness of Google.

A 1-to-1 device initiative can provide a platform to re-engage with the parent body and begin a new era of communication and collaboration. Providing a device that will enter the home levels the playing field for communication and opens up a number of possibilities. Indeed, alongside the suggested methodology above, a school could use the opportunity to change the way they communicate to parents full stop!

As suggested, the enhanced communication begins with initial presentations to the parent body about the 1-to-1 initiative. Whilst this might be perceived as a potential minefield of disgruntled parents with axes to grind, if handled correctly, it can enhance communication and foster positive relationships.

As there will be so many questions from parents, there is a strong argument that the big information evening we've just described should take a different, more inclusive form so all families feel they are being listened to. Take a typical year group of 150 students: the 1-to-1 programme could be launched across five meetings at different times of the working week to help parents fit around their normal schedule. For example: Monday, Tuesday, Thursday 6-7.30pm, Wednesday 7-8.30pm & Friday 1-2.30pm.

Taking a maximum of 35 parents for any meeting slot this will allow all parents to have their say and ask specific questions. It might seem labour intensive compared to one or two mass events, particularly when rolled out across an entire school. However, this schedule dramatically reduces the time required for separate meetings and email correspondence. Both methods have been shown to work across the authors' schools; it very much depends on context and capacity. For example, in the schools where Dominic ran a 1-to-1 project, getting parents to attend any event was challenging, so a large-scale, publicity blitz approach worked. In Dan's schools, serving a very different demography with very different attitudes to consultation, the small class-by-class method was the only way to go.

Moreover, this interaction on a smaller scale provides an opportunity for the parental body to engage with the school about learning centred around a whole school initiative. Of course there will still be the 'bottom 5%' who want to argue the case for no devices. However, if the school have decided to move to a 1-to-1 programme, the more parents that are on board the simpler the task will be. Parents may also understand a little more about the way their child will learn with their device. This will reap rewards a little further down the line when attempting to support their child with the learning process. Seeing them in action during a workshop can remove a number of barriers to support, with the parents otherwise feeling out of touch with the technology.

This increased engagement with the parent body can then lead to enhanced communication through digital correspondence. A regular newsletter is strongly recommended, with access guaranteed through the student's device. If the family don't have Internet capability at home, the newsletter can be downloaded by the student at school. Similarly, increasing the students' capability with technology at school can help them support parents to access information at home. Linking an email account to a smartphone or accessing payment options via the school website can be instigated by the child. Encouraging parents to access correspondence is tricky for all schools from time to time. The 1-to-1 initiative provides an opportunity to stimulate engagement.

To take this communication a stage further, the 1-to-1 programme can also provide a platform for parents to access and pose questions about their child's progress. As the workflow becomes digitised and stored in the cloud, this allows teachers to grant access to various stakeholders. Take the previously mentioned Edmodo, the free platform that can host homework, grades and school notices. A pupil code can be shared with parents that allows them to view everything from assigned work to interactions between students and teachers. This access can be granted on an individual or class level depending on the content a school wishes parents to access. Immediately this means parents can come to parent-teacher conferences with increased knowledge, allowing that precious ten minute talk to contain more substance. it also involves the parents more in their child's learning and can help to paint a clearer picture when teachers phone home. The presence of digital badges also allows praise to be visible and easily identified once the parents are used to the system. They no longer have to wait for termly reports or meetings.

These communication platforms have also made it into the profit making sector of education with solutions available to bring together a host of school services. These solutions are well worth looking into as they may streamline already paid for options. To give one example of this, take the Realsmart platform that has gained traction across the UK.

Realsmart offers:

- Google Apps for Education (GAFE) setup and domain register;
- MIS synchronisation;
- Blog setup and other organisational structures;
- Folder structure from permissions to settings (YouTube, Google+, Chat);
- Single Sign On to third party websites through smartpass;
- GAFE training;
- The ability to share and celebrate learning through the website/ portal;
- Personalised accounts for everyone.

It is worth an initial meeting with this type of company to compare the cost of a new product to the on-going internal costs already incurred. The focus should be on a clear, defined platform that is easy to use for teachers, students & parents. Get it right and the communication with all stakeholders is simpler and therefore more likely to engage.

7.3.2   eSafety, management of devices and behaviour support

The impact of introducing a device into the family environment and subsequent eSafety concerns can't be underestimated. Even with web filtering and device controls, many parents will be concerned either because they don't understand it or don't know how to control it. Therefore a school must do all it can to allay fears and offer support. This support should come from every stakeholder. Reassurance from the Headteacher as well as advice from the lead teacher are particularly useful approaches. Often a parent just needs to discuss their concerns and be shown what they can do. For those with limited technological experience, they have probably worked hard to isolate their household from digital stuff for years and you've just disrupted all of that.

The main thing to remember when it come to online safety is that it is ever-evolving and there should be an acceptance that it is impossible to filter, block and control every aspect of a student's online experience. This is not to lay blame at any individual or system failures, rather that it is very easy to connect a device to unfiltered Wi-Fi in public areas and students are savvy when it comes to accessing apps or content that they desire.

Therefore, eSafety is more about education than control. Liken it to the 'don't talk to strangers' message we all learn as children. A child knows that they shouldn't speak to strangers through education of the dangers. They still walk past strangers every day in the street, they just don't engage with them. There is much greater risk in totally insulating someone from reality and then letting them loose on it aged 18, than slowly and advisedly teaching them to recognise and avoid risk for themselves from an early age.

It is our duty to educate students, with the help of parents, about the dangers of online content and communication. Of course there will be filtering and control on our Wi-Fi networks at home and in school. However, the education should be aimed at warning signs and no-go areas online, much like it does in other aspects of our life-skills education.

There are a couple of things worth remembering about Internet filtering and monitoring. Schools should inform all students that filtering of content exists for their safety and monitoring: "Yes we can see content you have accessed" is there to ensure the AUP is being followed. Whilst a school doesn't require consent to filter and monitor the Internet, they should inform users that it is happening, to maintain trust. Therefore this should be part of communication to parents and students and as such is worth including in the Acceptable Use Policy.

A school eSafety programme should cover a number of different aspects of online safety:

- How to use technology and the Internet safely;
- How to ignore and report inappropriate material;
- What types of behaviour online can lead to greater risks;
- The type of risks other children and adults can pose;

- What a child should do if they are exposed to bullying or grooming online;
- If in doubt, who a child can speak to.

The school should maintain a regular dialogue with all its stakeholders to ensure everyone is kept informed of developments in the online world. A simple parent/ student survey can quickly engage the community and provide data to help with decisions moving forward. Likewise, placing an eSafety newsletter into the school's regular communications can act as a reminder to maintain vigilance.

When launching a 1-to-1 device initiative, it is certain that top of a parent's agenda will be online safety and the protection of their children. eSafety should be part of any FAQ pack and presenters at any information evening should be very clear about the procedures the school will put in place. The PSHE coordinator should be aware of the on-going requirement for eSafety updates to be included and appropriate time given to its importance. Every teacher should be well versed in eSafety guidelines. Online pastoral issues will increase over time and it is important that a consistent message is heard by parents and students.

To help educate students and parents there are a number of different organisations who specialise in eSafety and provide online courses. These are regularly updated to keep abreast of on-going developments. It is worthwhile taking a look at:

- CEOP - www.thinkuknow.co.uk
- Kidsmart - www.kidsmart.org.uk
- BBC - www.bbc.co.uk/cbbc/topics/stay-safe
- E-safety Support - www.e-safetysupport.com

Support for parents should also include practical advice for the home environment. Include tips advising the best way to apply their ISP's web filters to common home wireless systems and point them in the right direction when it comes to the latest advice. Open DNS is always a useful starting point for those parents with tricky home systems: http://www.opendns.com/.

Most importantly, help them with parental controls for the device their child is using. As well as offering information packs and perhaps a parents evening, workshops are very useful. This allows parents to understand that they have the power to 'control' access to certain apps and content and be hands on with the device. They will also value the time available to discuss issues they may be having. These issues can be as simple as what rules should be in place at home. Whilst no teacher would ever advise on how to parent a child, there are a couple of suggestions that are usually well received:

- The device is never allowed in the bedroom, unless that is where the child works;
- The device is always charged overnight in a communal space;
- Work to be completed is cross referenced with recorded homework tasks.

There will always be plenty of free advice for parents on how to make sure their child is safe online. It is our job as teachers to point the parents in the right direction and provide opportunities for discussion, particularly when implementing a 1-to-1 programme. Directing energy to the workshops and supporting resources at the start of the programme will reap dividends later on in the process.

8 DEPLOYMENT

As with any whole-school initiative, the success of deployment day depends on the planning process. From school infrastructure capability to student input, any failing in the system can lead to a failed deployment, negative publicity and damage to your/ the project's credibility.

Deployment is also surprisingly poorly understood, even by device suppliers. Currently, there is a very definite set of actions which need to be followed in order to ready an iPad for deployment (Apple Configurator > Supervised Mode > Managed Deployment enrolment > MDM enrolment > VPP) but schools are too often left to work this out for themselves (after getting it wrong first). By the time you read this, that list will have undoubtedly have changed, but it serves as an example of the complexity of the issue. It would be really galling, wouldn't it, to work so hard on a great 1-to-1 project which suffers only one blip - and for that blip to be the bit that's visible to all the parents and children as their first experience of mobile learning. In summary, do your homework on deployment to avoid extra work, recalls and embarrassment.

There are many aspects to consider and school context is, as ever, very important:

- Infrastructure - Ensure wireless signal and incoming bandwidth can meet the demands of deployment and on-going use. Consider hardwired options for device deployment if the network may struggle. A caching server should be considered to help with bandwidth issues if the school is deploying a suite of applications as well as enrolment;

- Deployment Model - A school should chose a model that suits its context. Even with the most up to date infrastructure, it will take users time to complete the process. Prepare for a number of days where students will be available for deployment to alleviate the pressure on bandwidth. With the best will in the world, deploying more than 300 devices in a single day is tricky, not because of the technology but because of the individuals and any troubleshooting that may be required. If in doubt, a school year group each day is manageable and leaves time for issues to be dealt with;

- Mobile Device Management - As discussed in the MDM section, how the devices are managed is very important. The MDM allows everything to be managed in one place which means the devices don't have to be collected in for updating. The MDM will also help with enrolment and app deployment if required;

- Individual Device Management - Every device will need to be identified for a number of reasons, management, security, acceptable use. Again an MDM will help you with both identifying use and registering the device under a specific name or number (device serial numbers are very useful here). For the user, device identification should be clear. Consider stickers or engraving and make sure the device is easily identifiable when it is inside the protective case;

- Application purchase - Some device solutions will require the purchase of apps. Others will require logins to a browser-based solution. Ensure that the method of purchase and subsequent management has a sustainable solution in place. For example, apps can be purchased for iPad via the Volume Purchasing Programme. These app codes can then be pushed to specific devices via the MDM solution. The enrolled devices can then be set to automatically download purchased apps without the user having to do anything. Do you want this to happen all at the same time when devices are deployed? Again consider a caching server that will help to reduce bandwidth by locally storing the content;

- Login Details - Perhaps the most important piece of information for the individual user. If they are going to login to a Google Apps for Education (GAFE) domain, or sign in with an Apple ID, how is that going to be communicated and managed on-going? It's recommended that the initial GAFE login is a generic password that then syncs using Google Apps Sync across the domain. This means that a student will have the same password for mail and other Google services. For app purchases on iPad the user requires an Apple ID at the moment. It is recommended that the school creates the Apple IDs for the student using their school email as the login name - you will need to get Apple to whitelist your school for this to be technically possible. Passwords are all stored within the domain or MDM solution and easily accessible to IT staff. As the student has more control of the technology with a personal device, it is often forgotten passwords that provide a stumbling block. On deployment day, have a member of staff overseeing any initial login process and password verification.

A typical deployment scenario could look like this:

Preparation
- Unbox and tag the device for school and user identification;
- Create login credentials for each user - GAFE, Office365, Apple ID;
- Assign devices in MDM solution/ Domain;
- Configure enrolment to install accounts, settings, restrictions. If possible this should be a wireless solution;
- Send any invitations to each device, for example, VPP codes for apps. Assign the codes to the individual device using MDM;
- We won't go into anything more specific than this list, as the deployment method for each device and ecosystem changes so rapidly. For example, by the time you read this Apple may well have released their Device Enrolment Program (DEP), which is currently making a big difference to deployments in the States.

On the day

- When handed the device the student should be helped to enter login details and check password security;
- The device should be checked for settings and configurations received from the MDM or that the login grants access to required domain usage;
- Each student should accept any invitation from the MDM or domain and install/ download applications as appropriate. If a device is in Supervised Mode this will be automatic.

The room for deployment should be set up as a carousel to speed up the hand-out and management process. It is worth dedicating a separate space for troubleshooting and also app downloads. Ideally, app downloading should be pushed out to students' home broadband (e.g. scheduled to kick in at the weekend). Even if the school is using a caching server, it will take time to download all the content. Again, it is worth considering that an initial deployment may take time as users get used to the process. Leave time between groups for any backlog to be dealt with.

Paperwork requirements can also be built into this deployment carousel. Many schools ask parents to come and collect the device with their child. If so this is where the AUP can be signed and any financial arrangements that need to be finalised. Similarly, this is an excellent time for a school leader to emphasise acceptable use and good practice. A brief talk followed by the signing of the official student AUP can work very well as a line in the sand. Whilst not wanting to dampen enthusiasm, it is crucial the students understand the device is for learning and misuse and breakages can severely hamper the learning process. It may also be necessary to confirm the identity of the parent and take a photograph (using one of the devices, obviously!) of the tablet/ laptop being handed over.

For large scale deployments with a limited timeframe the situation can be a little different. It is recommended that the school set up a number of caching servers to deal with bandwidth demand. Login and profile acceptance will still take a little time and any delays are amplified with large numbers of devices handed out at once. Schools should consider setting aside a day to complete the process on the understanding it will continue after normal school hours. This will allow for any issues to be dealt with, where possible, so it doesn't affect the child's learning. It also means that troubleshooting can occur when there is less demand on the network.

As with any whole school initiative, a large scale deployment is more likely to succeed when the preparation has been as detailed as possible. The less the end user has to do to get up and running, the easier it will be. There is still the likelihood that troubleshooting will be required the following day so build time into the schedule and make staff understand other support services may be restricted for a short time. Again the advice would be, if you are deploying hundreds of devices, try to stagger them across a few days rather than deploy them all at once.

8.2.1   Security and software considerations

When deploying any device in school it is worth considering a number of different security issues that may crop up when handling the devices. Not least of which is what will happen with the devices from when they are received by the school prior to deployment day. It is very important the school reviews its insurance policy and has a secure place to store the devices overnight or possibly longer. Whilst it would be ideal from a security perspective to receive the devices the day before deployment, this will not be practical for the IT team who need to asset tag and configure each device. Ask a retailer/ reseller to advise through this process as they will have handled it a number of times for schools with a similar context. A secure storage space would ideally be lockable, alarmed, covered by CCTV, above ground floor level, with no windows; server rooms often get used.

Security of the students should also be considered on deployment day. Whilst the day to day management of the device should be covered by your AUP, it won't necessarily apply on the first day. There will be a level of excitement and the students will be keen to use the device and show friends outside of school. It's important to state that the student should not remove the device from their bag whilst travelling home and shouldn't openly display the device when out in public. It is a learning tool and as such only needs to be used in school or at home in most cases. There is a tricky balancing act between maintaining a positive experience for the students on deployment day and enforcing acceptable use. It's worth having a couple of teachers manning the school gates to remind students as they leave.

It is also recommended that devices are deployed on a Friday to allow the initial excitement to calm down over the weekend. This means the students will get used to the device and come to school on Monday a little less keen to try every single app they can get their hands on. This is only a suggestion as the counter argument to this is the student has to wait two days if there are any problems with configuration or settings. Again the context of the school is important.

If any devices are to stay in school then it is essential to invest in a secure storage solution that allows charging. Following the initial deployment it impossible that some students will only access their device in school due to family wishes or school policy. If this is likely to be the case then insurance, security and charging will need to be considered. The risk of organised theft is significant in some schools, particularly if you have gained publicity for your project. On deployment day(s), make sure the large numbers of devices you have ready to hand out are stored somewhere lockable and separate from the general deployment activity, in case of problems. For example, one school we have worked with also invited the local PCSO to attend and quarantined the devices from the attendees of the deployment event, using a voucher system to confirm identity and then allow the collection of a device from a second nearby location. In that context, these were sensible precautions which caused limited issues.

There is also the issue of age appropriate security for use of software by children under the age of 13. On deployment day the school must be clear that all appropriate permissions have been granted for the student to use their device. For example, Apple now have an Apple ID for Students programme that is designed for students under the age of 13. The Apple IDs are requested by the school to be registered to it and will only be created by Apple once verifiable consent has been given by a parent or guardian. The Parent Privacy Disclosure and consent form must be signed. For these students, iCloud email is deactivated and no advertisement tracking is permitted by Apple.

Similarly, the school shouldn't deploy any apps that are deemed 17+ to any students. This is because whilst there may be 18 year old students in the school, this will not be true for an entire class. An age appropriate solution should be deployed dependant on the learning objective, regardless of how popular an app is.

It is a good idea to deploy devices with suggested educational apps from the chosen manufacturer. Both Apple and Google have excellent educational app recommendations built into their stores. From Google's point of view the 'Chrome App Packs for Education' is superb with more than enough variety to suit the needs of teachers and students alike. These apps also come recommended by teachers from around the world who have been using them everyday to support the learning process in 1-to-1 schools.

Apple have an Education section on their app store that has recommendations by subject and age range. Again these apps come recommended by teachers and the Education section should be regularly visited for the latest app releases that support learning. Fortunately, any new iPad now comes free with the iWork and iLife suite of apps that are perfect for starting out with a 1-to-1 iPad programme. The apps included in these suites support all the functionality you would expect and give immediate access to image, video and audio capture. This means that the iPad will immediately allow teachers to change some of the learning objectives with student video and audio recording part of the process. iWork contains your standard 'office productivity' apps for word processing, spreadsheets and presentations.

8.2.2 Suggested initial apps for a 1-to-1 iPad deployment

When deciding on which applications to buy for teachers and students, ignore the temptation to buy content or glitz, concentrate on applications that help with productivity, that foster effective research, that enable creative outcomes, and those that support teaching processes across the board rather than in specific subjects.

Make sure to utilise volume purchasing schemes. Apple's VPP, although deeply annoying to set up and use, brings a 50% saving on qualifying apps (not all do) when you buy 20 licences or more. They keep promising to allow the use of Purchase Orders in the UK, but at the time of writing payment is only by credit card or via a strange German version of PayPal.

Ensure that there are some quick wins for teachers. After all, they need compelling reasons to alter their practice, beyond the sheer force of your personality. A good start is finding a way to do the simple things (like take a register, look up a pupil's contact details) without recourse to the full MIS via a PC. The substantial investment needed for apps from SIMS or Groupcall Emerge pays itself off in goodwill and 'aha' moments pretty quickly.

The following list of recommended apps changes less often than you'd think:

Explain Everything

Simply the most versatile education app available. Explain Everything is an interactive whiteboard and screen-casting tool that suits the needs of teachers and students alike. The app allows you to animate, annotate and narrate presentations and explanations to your audience. It is widely used to record plenaries and provide audio feedback. It is also the app of choice for students when they are required to provide more than written material. The key to its success can found in its intuitive interface and export options. A 'must have' app in education.

Socrative 2.0

Socrative is a very simple and effective assessment tool that can be used during any part of the learning process. A teacher can pose questions to a group which they answer on their device with the information directly relayed back to the host. It is available as long as there is an Internet connection. The most common use for Socrative is as an 'exit ticket' for a lesson. Students answer four or five questions at the end of a lesson so the teacher has feedback to base the next lesson on. All data is sent directly to the teacher's email account as soon as they end the quiz. Very useful for planning.

iMovie

iMovie has always been a favourite with students, but it is interesting to see how it has developed as an educational tool. As well as an obvious movie creation and editing app, iMovie provides a platform to express learning. The 'trailer' option guides students to capture snapshots to show learning as well as to input text to frame their ideas. These trailers then serve as interesting starter videos or revision tools. iMovie projects take over where a student or teacher may want to add greater depth.

iTunes U

iTunes U is often referred to as a learning platform. iTunes U courses provide the framework and resources so teachers can get on with what they do best. Removing the need for photocopying, Internet searching and distribution, iTunes U supports a culture of creation and collaboration. The value of having access to everything required on one device can't be underestimated and its popularity is growing by the day. Add to this the ability to update any resource and make it available to all at the tap of a screen and you have a very powerful learning platform.

Showbie

Showbie allows you to assign, collect and review student work. As a tool it meets a demand that used to be supplied by a school VLE. The difference here is the ability to 'open in' a multitude of apps to create content or provide feedback. A couple of taps sees a student assignment opened and annotated with audio feedback or viewed in the teacher's app of choice. It is then just as simple to return the assignment to the student for immediate viewing. Showbie works very well with larger classes where the transfer of information is frequent.

Edmodo

Edmodo fulfils the need for a collaboration and communication tool within the school environment. The secure site is suitable as nobody can gain access to a group without the unique code. Many students use Edmodo to question their peers over challenging questions and as a platform to collaborate on projects. It is interesting to see how groups communicate under the tutelage of a teacher. Edmodo is also used as a tool to model good practice on the Internet. For many students it is their first interaction with social media in a controlled environment and Edmodo has proved a very useful component of many eSafety programmes.

Notability

As a note taking app, Notability stands out from the crowd. With all the tools available to record information, Notability is a real favourite with students. The most common use can be seen as students take a picture of a resource or experiment and then jot down information to highlight key terms. The export functions within Notability also make it suitable for students as they develop their digital portfolios.

Keynote

Keynote is the presentation tool of choice for students, particularly when faced with a class or school presentation. Students are very positive about the ease with which they can convey a message using multimedia. There is distinct attention paid to the use of transitions to emphasise a point and interestingly an engagement with the requirements of the future world of work. Students often equate job applications and progress with presentations so using Keynote to express learning is very desirable. Ask a student to convey something that they have learned, and it is likely to be Keynote they turn to first.

Book Creator

From simple projects to a school term's worth of learning, Book Creator has become a handy vessel for curation and creation. With the ability to add video to explanations as well as 'widget' type effects, students of all ages enjoy using Book Creator. It deserves its inclusion due to the ease with which all tools can be used and the wide range of export functions available. Stand-alone projects are ably supported by Book Creator as it acts as a working portfolio to document the learning process.

Pages

Pages is simply a 'go to' app of choice when students are asked to produce a piece of written work, as it has been the iPad's Word-equivalent for years. There are further layers to the app though that enhance the learning process. Firstly, the templates remove the need to spend time over layout and formatting. When the task requires a student to convey their learning, time is no longer wasted on making the document look good. Secondly, the multimedia aspect of Pages elevates it as a document creator. As well as the written word, students submit photos and video to support their views, all professionally laid out.

There are a multitude of apps that could make this list and schools may wish to consider adding to the portfolio without overloading the users. It is interesting how 'top' apps are usually generic in nature and that they allow teachers and students to be creative with their use. Of course there will always be subject specific apps that enhance learning. However, initial app deployment should be based on scarcity and familiarity to help teachers, parents and students cope with all this new information. As a benchmark, more than twenty apps is overwhelming and not recommended.

9 EVALUATING IMPACT

Section 9.1 Awww! Do I have to? Can't I just go out and play?

As you will no doubt be aware, education is currently in the grip of a fevered debate about the importance of evidence. 'Evidence-based policy making' was a phrase constantly on the lips of the most recent ex-Secretary of State, with the rhetoric suggesting we've all be blundering around in the dark until now. The 'conversation' (though it seems like more of a fight sometimes) revolves around two points of view;

The first is that held by, arguably, most people working in schools and it runs like this; it is down to teachers to use their professional judgement to decide what will work best for their children, in their context. After all, they see every day the thousands of tiny steps forward taken by children as a result of effective teaching. In short, teachers know what works. We wouldn't characterise it as an 'anti-evidence' stance - we've never yet met a teacher who didn't want to find out about even better methods and employ them in their own classroom - but it's definitely a position which places greater value on the teacher's own experience of education.

The alternate position is somewhat more fundamentalist, and is championed most often by those who are not working in schools, or so it seems from this fence on which we are currently rather awkwardly sat.

Their position can be described thus; without methodologically-sound, quantitative evidence of a causal relationship between an intervention and improved learning outcomes, no one can say that anything works. Without evidence, all you have is a hunch, or a prejudice you are trying to confirm. And you certainly shouldn't spend £500k (see Section 4.1) on a hunch or a prejudice. It's an empiricism that frequently likens schools to medicine or the physical sciences.

We firmly believe that there is room for both of these mind-sets inside the great tent of education, and that a middle ground exists - something José calls 'evidence-informed rather than evidence-driven teaching'. However, suggesting this to any committed proponent of either camp usually results in accusations of heresy and firewood being stacked in the middle of the town square. The debate has, sadly, become very polarised and each side has its fair share of mad-eyed zealots.

Now, we are telling you all this for a reason, not just for the sheer entertainment to be wrung from the discipline of educational epistemology (and boy, there's a lot of that). That reason is because at some stage in your 1-to-1 project you are going to need to demonstrate evidence of the impact of your intervention, so the preceding paragraphs serve as a useful backdrop to the field on which you will have to do battle. If your project is to be sustained beyond the first couple of years, you will need to justify to the powers that be (SLT, Governors) that it's worth sustaining.

Section 9.2 How to go about it

Do you want the good news or the bad news first? OK, we'll start with the bad; you are going to need to begin your evaluation of impact right from the start of the project. We know that sounds unappealing; the start should be all about the sexy cool stuff, like trialling new devices, shouldn't it? Yes it should, but this is education and there's always a price to pay for doing anything novel. Sorry, but if you are going to be able demonstrate progress, and to accurately ascribe it to this project, you need to think about it from the beginning and start collecting baseline data. If you don't, at best you'll have a bolted-on evaluation that makes what it can of the evidence available. At worst, you'll have missed the chance to understand and share something of genuine value. It's never too early to start thinking about how to do this.

But we did also mention good news, and that wasn't just a distraction tactic. It really is quite good news too: unless you are the super-ambitious type and have access to multiple schools, your research does not have to be generalisable. You are under precisely zero pressure to prove that your project would have the same effect if implemented elsewhere, you just need to show what impact it is having in your school. This relieves you of a bunch of tedious and difficult stuff, like randomisation, control groups, adjusting for various social-science no-nos like the Hawthorne effect. Obviously, it would be quite helpful if, in the course of your own evaluation, you could somehow demonstrate a reliably generalisable effect which would finally resolve the question mark hanging over technology's efficacy in learning for everyone… but if you can't, it's no biggie.

So don't worry, you do not have to design a double-blind Randomised Control Trial (RCT) or write a 10,000 word literature study as a preamble to the main findings, and no Peer is going to Review what you write. You are going to create **a mixed methods case study**, the aim of which is to show the impact (or lack thereof) of *your* 1-to-1 project in *your* school.

Your job is not to examine the impact of technology - it is to establish the impact of your implementation of technology, and these are two separate things. The first implies that if you take the treatment (technology) and apply it anywhere, it will make a discernable difference. This is clearly nonsense. Becta spent fifteen years and millions of taxpayers' pounds in pursuit of this, and look what happened to them. The second, more reasonable and achievable approach says 'This thing (technology), implemented in this way, in this place, has led to these changes…'.

Let's talk about what we can and can't reliably measure within a single-school piece of research, to start with.

9.2.1 Quantitative data

This is what people mean when they talk about 'hard' data. Quantitative evidence is evidence based on statistical analysis of things that can be counted. There are lots of things that can be counted in a school, we're sure you can think of a most of them without our help. The number of things that can be counted AND shown to be sensitive to the application of technology interventions are, however, vanishingly few.

This is not due to the ineffectiveness of said interventions (though we can't rule that out), but rather because its really hard to separate out the effect of *anything* in an environment as complex and constantly changing as a school, without using tools like RCTs, which are almost impossible to implement within a single institution.

For example, let's say your 1-to-1 seems to be a stunning success. The staffroom is abuzz every lunchtime with talk of Explain Everything, the children are routinely doing school work collaboratively in the evenings and Mr Spargle, the 40-year veteran of the Maths department, has applied to become an ADE. Your GCSE results come in and, wouldn't you know it, you've beaten your best ever 5 A*-C total by 10%.

That 10% is a quantitative measure, but it may be a measure of lots of things. It could be the result of the Behaviour for Learning strategy, put in place three years ago finally bearing fruit. It could be the impact of an exceptional head of Year 11 who has moved with this cohort over the last five years. It could be something experimental the council is putting in the local water supply. Or all of this and 17 other things too. Because you haven't identified and adjusted for these other factors, they are in the way of you getting a clear view of what's going on. You've no credible way of proving it has anything to do with your 1-to-1 project. In fact, it would be just as valid to suggest that 1-to-1 has retarded what would otherwise have been a 15% gain...

You can hypothesise and assert, but you cannot prove much with blunt instruments like exam results unless you design a study that manages to isolate the particular needle of your 1-to-1 intervention in a classroom-sized pile of other needles, and then measure unequivocally how sharp it is. That would need a really effective RCT, and one spread across a much wider population than can be provided by one school.

The problem with RCTs is that they're very hard to do well in education, for lots of reasons. We'll leave the debate over the ethics of control groups aside and focus purely on the reality of most school-based research – and that's the fact that it tends to be opportunistic and reflect pre-existing structures. Most often the intervention (in this case, the use of 1-to-1) is designed primarily with logistical and educational concerns in mind and any research study has to fit around this.

Randomisation of treatment/ control groups, so crucial to removing the obscuring veil of other factors, is almost never the starting point. For practical reasons, groups are usually formed using existing classes of pupils, which are very un-random in their nature (this is called 'clustering' in methodological terms). It's hard to imagine a school putting randomisation of groups in a study ahead of all the other things they have to do in order to function properly.

Also, as children get older, the range between the highest and lowest achievement grows (the 'standard deviation'), making it harder to statistically demonstrate impactful interventions, which only show up clearly outside the margins of this. So there's some reason to doubt RCT's ability to deliver impressive results in secondary education. Not to be negative, but if you're in a single school context and have no wider need to provide generalisable evidence, you should abandon the idea of establishing a causal, statistical link between your 1-to-1 project and attainment.

This is not to say that you should give up on quantitative data full stop, just that you should have a realistic view on what it can prove for you. If we narrow the focus a little, it can still tell us useful things. For example, if you were to look at progress rather than terminal achievement this would allow you to see what's going on over time in year groups that don't sit public exams and it would provide data that is comparable across year groups, which could be useful as a control. More on this below.

9.2.2 Qualitative data

This is sometimes labelled 'soft' data. Qualitative research aims to get behind and beyond the numbers to understand how and why something has happened - it's gathered by asking people about what they've experienced.

The main criticism of qualitative evidence is its lack of rigour - when broken down into individual pieces of data, it's really just the opinion of a single person. That single person has prejudices, history and a limit to their understanding of the thing they're being asked about. Basically, just reporting what they say is a vox pop, not research. It can tell you about how something has had a perceived effect, but can't prove if it *actually* has.

This doesn't mean qualitative data isn't extremely revealing in the right circumstances. If the respondents (the people whose opinions are being sought) are representative of the wider school population, diverse and have been discouraged from just saying what they think you want to hear, then they can tell you things about your project that you could not otherwise understand. Qualitative methods are great at finding out how 1-to-1 has had an effect on what it feels like to be at your school, on how children are learning, on which subjects are making most effective use of these tools, et cetera.

And it doesn't have to remain 'soft' data. If you ask enough people for their view, define some structure for the types of things they say (this is called 'coding') and count up the frequency with which these codes occur, you have effectively quantified the qualitative, turning a bunch of opinions into meaningful numbers which demonstrate trends. Within a single school, perceptions of impact are, effectively, real impact. It may be a localised effect due purely to the quality of implementation rather than the technology itself but so what? It's working.

Section 9.3 A good structure for a credible mixed methods study

Let's restate the thrust of the previous couple of pages: the aim of your evaluation study is to understand what impact your 1-to-1 project is having on your students and their learning, not to provide final, clinching proof of the efficacy of technology per se.

With that in mind, you will want to understand a couple of things - 1. Is this intervention making a difference to the pace of students' progress? 2. Is it changing what it's like to learn and be at this school? These are very different questions and require different sources of data, and these are the 'mixed' methodologies referred to in the heading above. For a case study, mixed methods are totally acceptable and will provide a much more nuanced and detailed view of your project than pure quantitative or qualitative approaches alone. Another advantage is that if these mixed sources of data are collected intelligently, you should be able to use them for 'triangulation'. This is another research term, this time borrowed from orienteering - triangulation means finding out where you are by comparing the position of two things that you can see.

9.3.1   Stats

Starting with the question of progress, you are going to need to have two measures; one a baseline (starting point, ideally carried out before the intervention) and the second taken a decent time after the change has bedded in. In most cases, you will probably use Teacher Assessment grades carried out at the end of the school year. For example, take the point scores for every subject for every student at the end of Year 7 as your baseline, and then measure how much progress these children make in Year 8.

The reason we suggest using Year 8 as your sample is for a number of reasons. Firstly, there is the issue of diminishing returns from standard deviation in older students (see above - it just gets harder to see the differences as the range of performance widens). Secondly, if they've already been in your school for a year, you'll have more reliable internal data (e.g. every maths assessment will be consistently marked, as opposed to those carried out in Y6 across several different feeder schools). Finally and most importantly, using Year 8 helps you to control for the 'school effect'. This is a catch-all term for the impact seen on performance from the myriad factors that go into making your school such a success (your ethos, the Head's munificence, the quality of the turkey twizzlers, et cetera). If we were using the recently arrived Year 7 cohort, it would be valid to dismiss any positive finding as just being the result of the school effect; of all the other stuff that these children are experiencing in a new setting. By using Year 8, we can adjust for that, because you know how much progress they made last year and can compare that with this year. In that way, whatever the general school effect is, you should be able to see if your 1-to-1 project made a difference above and beyond.

Using Teacher Assessments is more reliable than it sounds too. Generally, the quality of these judgements will remain stable year to year, something which cannot be said of exam thresholds. Because you're looking at the whole population of a year group (or two if you want to extend your study), any inconsistencies between teachers or classes should be evened out. It really doesn't matter if you don't have much faith in the History department's ability to assess students' learning. As long as they continue to be as poor as you suspect them to be, their assessment remains a consistent measure you can use. We're being facetious - the History department is always awesome. It's the Geographers who you need to watch out for.

Teacher Assessment also gives you access to a really broad range of measures, rather than the narrower field provided by exam results or other cognitive tests and looking at progress in all subjects can be a real eye-opener as to which departments are really making the most of the affordances of the technology. Triangulated with the qualitative data we'll talk about below, you can learn a lot from this.

Another good way to reveal the impact of your project is to look at historic data. Carry out the same analysis (progress in all subjects from end of Year 7 to end of Year 8) on the last three cohorts. Average out all three into one score and you will then have an average points of progress number which describes how much progress students in Year 8 in your school typically make. Comparing this with the same aggregated number for the current cohort who have had the treatment may result in a positive differential. One fairly robust interpretation of this differential is that it's the impact of your 1-to-1. This isn't a perfect science, as you don't really know what happened in past years and major school improvements may have taken place since then, but because we're focussed on progress rather than attainment, it's as steady a measure as is likely to exist.

These 'historic control groups', whilst flawed because of other factors that may have been at play, could be further strengthened by creating a contemporary control, if circumstances allow. Most 1-to-1 projects have a staggered roll-out for one reason or another, so plan to take advantage of this. If there's a year group (let's say Year 9 here) who are not getting the intervention for another academic year, you can repeat exactly the same analysis (progress made this year, compared against progress made in Years 8 and 7, alongside the average progress of historic Year 9 cohorts). This gives you perhaps the cleanest, clearest view of the impact of your project, as these children are subject to exactly the same factors as your treatment group, minus the treatment. The only confounding variable is the difference in maturity and history (they're older, and they've been through a slightly longer and different experience).

9.3.2   Surveys and interviews

Having done your detailed analyses of progress described above, you now have a pretty strong quantitative evidence base for impact on progress. What you don't yet have is any reliable source of information about *why* this impact exists, and in what other ways the project is creating change. For that, you're going to need to access the views of those on the receiving end.

There are two interrelated ways of doing this with minimum effort for maximum return - and it starts with a 'pre-test' survey of everyone in the treatment and control groups (Year 8 and Year 9, in the example we've been building). The point of this survey is two fold - to establish a baseline, as with the progress stats, and to identify interesting respondents to interview. You should do it with treatment and control groups for the same reasons that you're gathering qualitative data from both - to see if through comparison you can reveal any differences.

There are a couple of things that we think you would be wise to be aware of and to adjust for. One is 'confirmation bias', which is where the researcher, unconsciously or otherwise, designs a research instrument in such a way that it gathers data that supports their existing prejudices and theories. It's a subtle bias, exhibited usually in leading questions. The other is 'acquiescence bias', which is the tendency of respondents (and particularly prevalent in children) to agree with statements when they don't actually know, and to want to please the researcher by telling them what they think they want to hear.

To successfully counter both of these threats to your data's validity and usefulness, We suggest that you design a student survey that doesn't actually ask them about the thing you are researching, but rather focuses on issues of learning, motivation, challenge, the quality of teaching, the usefulness of homework tasks, et cetera. By separating the survey content from the treatment in this way, students' pre-existing positive biases towards technology will not influence their response. Put it this way; if you asked the question "Is the 1-to-1 project helping you to learn?', a lot of children would say 'yes' regardless of their (possibly unexamined) view, due to humans' proclivity to acquiesce. Others would say 'yes' because they enjoy using technology at school (and not always for the reasons you'd want them to) and don't want this to stop. What you're actually after, however, is some evidence that it's producing a change, so the approach of asking subjects about this treatment directly is likely to be counter-productive. No, we need to take a tangential path and sneak up on this.

In one study the authors have been involved in, while there were some passing references to technology, to allow better analysis of the responses, the questions were focussed on school life more generally, on the surface. If you considered the questions a bit more deeply though, you would have seen that they described aspects of learning and school life on which a successful 1-to-1 might be hypothesised to have an effect. Coming up with questions which achieve this whilst remaining in stealth mode is a real skill.

The easiest way to administer and analyse these surveys is through an online tool. There are lots out there, but we've always found www.SurveyMonkey.com hard to beat.

The questions in the sample make use of a four-point Likert scale, which uses a statement and invites the respondent to Strongly Agree, Agree, Disagree or Strongly Disagree with it. Having four choices removes the issue of 'gravitation towards the norm' (a phenomenon whereby most people go for the median value if given five or three choices) and forces respondents to get off the fence. It can also help you give confirmation bias the slip, if you mix up positive and negative statements when you write your survey. This is because respondents that just agree with every statement wind up being neutral overall. In our experience, it's best to avoid free-text fields in surveys - if you want detailed opinions, this isn't the best tool to access them (see below for that). You may want to use some multiple choice questions though, particularly if you are interested in seeing what students' views are of the approaches taken by different subjects.

The survey was referred to above as a 'pre-test' because it should be administered a couple of months before the treatment begins, so that your snapshot captures what the children thought about school without your 1-to-1 project influencing them at all.

It should be repeated as a 'post-test' at the same time you are collecting the quantitative measure of progress (e.g. at the end of Year 8 in the example we're using). This is where things start to get interesting. The simplest analysis to carry out is an aggregated view (e.g. as a percentage of the total) of how the treatment cohort's thinking about school has developed in the time between the tests, looking for significant changes. These changes are your first indication of where more detailed investigation may bear fruit. You will also want to compare the aggregated views of the treatment and the control group, which should show up differences which could be reasonably ascribed to the 1-to-1 project.

The next action is to look for students whose survey responses give particularly strong indications of a change in their thinking over the year. If possible, try to find six children with a mix of characteristics (ability, gender, social factors) and carry out paired, semi-structured interviews with them. You'll want a range of 'types' so that the data that results is as representative of the Year group as possible. The reason for pairs is that this removes the pressure of one-on-one conversations, but equally doesn't give the hiding places of a larger group. It can be useful to pair up a boy and a girl, preferably who already know each other. A 'semi-structured' interview is one in which the interviewer (you) has a list of topics rather than specific questions which must be answered, and allows the conversation to flow around them naturally.

The things you'll be interested in exploring with the students are the things that have caught your eye from the survey data. If the survey shows that over the year the homework tasks set by teachers have become more relevant, for example, you will want to hear about examples and try to uncover the reason why (which maybe, just maybe, has something to do with the awesome 1-to-1 programme you've introduced). An academic would tape record these interviews so that precise wording can be transcribe and cited, but this may be a layer of effort too far for your purposes and careful notes should suffice.

The data that you get from these interviews is gold dust, particularly as you can use their quotes it in any written evaluation of the project's impact, but you'll likely also have identified a group of interesting, interested and articulate students who you can use in the future to make your case.

A final interesting thing you can do with the survey data is a bit of the triangulation referred to a few pages back. If your survey asked for the students to enter their names, you can cross-analyse between the two data sources. For example, you might want to take the 20% of students whose survey responses show the most positive changes and see if this has translated into above average progress. This is a potentially very powerful way of showing that a well implemented 1-to-1 can positively impact on children of all ability levels, not just those who are already motivated and high-achieving.

If you have carried out all of the steps above, well done - you'll have amassed some really reliable and detailed data about how and to what extent your 1-to-1 project has impacted on your school and your students. It will be relatively simple from that point to produce a short written report combining the one-two punches of quantitative ('Ooh, look at that graph! 88% you say?') and qualitative ('What an amazing quote from Amie-Jo about how this has changed English for her!') evidence.

Section 9.4 Taking this further

We should say, despite all the tongue-in-cheek academia-poking above, if you are about to embark on a higher level degree with a research element (Masters or even a Doctorate, you masochist), then this project would be a great hook to hang your thesis off. It's chock-full of research questions (remember, no one knows *anything* according to the empiricists) and the studies to date leave a lot of room for improvement - low hanging fruit for an excoriating literature review.

And just as exciting, there would be the potential to reveal something quite robust if we all agreed on a similar research design and then pooled our results. This is called a meta-study and, if you can remove flawed studies (ones that have been poorly controlled or look at low-quality implementations), the sheer number of studies and participants acts as a control for other variables. The quality of Headteacher/ income of the demographic/ prior attainment/ amount of Amphetamine in the water supply and all the other local variables disappear into the background due to number of contexts involved.

That's why we're providing the facility via www.educate1to1.org/evidence to contribute data from your study to a wider analysis. Studies should broadly conform to the design set out in the section above - but what is more important is that the implementation of your 1-to-1 project is done well. But you know how to do that now, right?

Glossary

Android
A tablet and phone operating system designed by Google and used by many different tablet manufacturers, from Samsung's Galaxy Tab to Tesco's Hudl.

Chrome
Google's operating system which is used to run Chromebooks and as a cross-platform browser for any device. An essential part of their Apps for Education offering.

GAFE
Google Apps For Education - a suite of browser-based tools delivered through Chrome, free to schools. Productivity software, email, calendaring, online storage, video calling, the Classroom tool...

iOS
Apple's famously locked-down mobile operating system for iPad and iPhone. Big updates (iOS7, iOS8) routinely turn up the day after schools deploy devices in September...

iTunes U
Apple's content delivery mechanism, only accessible through a device running iOS. Used for creating and hosting multimedia courses, distributed and updated live to pupils.

MDM
Mobile Device Management - software that hooks into a device's operating system to allow the school to manage aspects of it. MDM lets you deploy apps, push wireless settings and restrict functions, all over the air without having to get the devices back.

Office365
Microsoft's online productivity/ email/ calendar/ storage suite, usually free to schools who already licence Office and Windows. Can connect your 1-to-1 project to the school's wider systems.

OSX
The 10th (the X is a Roman numeral) version of Apple's desktop operating system that runs on MacBooks and iMacs.

Workflow

The term used to describe a procedure for distributing work/ a task to pupils, allowing them to edit/ create and return it to the teacher. The goal is simplicity (fewest clicks) whilst maintaining flexibility and functionality.

ABOUT THE AUTHORS

Mark Baker (@say_mark) holds a technical position at The Hastings Academies Trust in East Sussex. He has worked in education his entire adult life and has progressed from technician to his current position as Head of ICT Services for a Multi-Academy Trust. During his career Mark has worked on a variety of challenging technical projects, including the design and implementation of the infrastructure for two new Academy buildings and the services which span them. With the experience of so many different sites and users, he has been able to adapt what he has learned to create an 1-to-1 infrastructure supporting hundreds of pupils across several sites in Hastings, UK.

Daniel Edwards (@syded06) is Director of Innovation & Learning at Stephen Perse Foundation schools, Cambridge, UK. He has taught physical education for over a decade and was a Director of Sport in a boys' grammar school in High Wycombe. Daniel implemented 1-to-1 device programmes for both of these schools and his current role centres around curriculum design and effective use of technology for learning. As an Apple Distinguished Educator and Apple Professional Development authorised trainer, Daniel regularly speaks at international conferences and runs training opportunities for teachers and school leaders across Europe.

Dominic Norrish (@domnorrish) is a former history teacher, school leader and Educational Technology consultant and is currently working as the Group Director of Technology at United Learning, a national group of over 50 maintained and independent schools. In this role he is responsible for the Group's technology strategy and most of his work revolves around helping schools to make effective use of technology for learning and ensuring that they benefit commercially from the Group's scale. Having joined United Learning from an Academy trust where he implemented a 1-to-1 strategy, Dominic is now involved in similar projects in several of his schools, utilising iPads, Chromebooks and Android tablets.

José Picardo (@josepicardoSHS) is Assistant Principal at Surbiton High School, where he leads on Digital Strategy. He has taught modern foreign languages for over ten years and regularly speaks at learning technologies and foreign languages themed conferences and training events, both nationally and internationally. In addition, José advises schools, government bodies and other organisations on the use of new and emerging technologies. He has devised and implemented his school's 1-to-1 strategy after having undertaken extensive research on the role of technology in supporting the processes involved in teaching and learning.

Adam Webster (@cagelessthink) is Director of Digital Learning at Caterham School. He is an English teacher who has made the transition to leading technology innovation in his school, leading their 1-to-1 initiative. As an Apple Distinguished Educator, he is heavily involved in training both staff and students in using mobile technology effectively. Adam's main focus has always been about marrying technology with teaching and learning, and he spends a great deal of time helping students and staff perfect the right workflows for being productive, effective and innovative.

8457835R00136

Printed in Great Britain
by Amazon.co.uk, Ltd.,
Marston Gate.